Soul Befriending

To Alice,

A woman of creative spirit, integrity, naKHinance, depth and laughter.

Happy Birthday,

Shine your Light Bright and hand out sunglasses to anyone who resists your light!

Love,
Rosie

Soul Befriending

High Beam Living and Loving

Rosalie Deer Heart

Copyright © 2014 by Rosalie Deer Heart

ISBN: 978-0-965157-69-8

All rights reserved. No part of this publication may be reproduced, stored in a retrieval system or transmitted, in any form, or by any means, electronic, mechanical, recorded, photocopied, or otherwise, without the prior written permission of both the copyright owner and the above publisher of this book, except by a reviewer who may quote brief passages in a review.

The scanning, uploading, and distribution of this book via the Internet or via any other means without the permission of the publisher is illegal and punishable by law. Please purchase only authorized electronic editions and do not participate in or encourage electronic piracy of copyrightable materials. Your support of the author's rights is appreciated.

Printed in the United States of America

Contents

Introduction 11

SECTION ONE: THE POWER OF STORIES
   Chapter One: Personal Story or Soul Story: Your Choice 17
   Chapter Two: Multi-Dimensional Nature of
      Consciousness and Beliefs 45
   Chapter Three: Releasing Resistance and Claiming Freedom 65

PART TWO: BRIDGING PERSONAL STORY AND SOUL STORY
   Chapter Four: Bridging Personal Story To Soul Story 87
   Chapter Five: Befriending Intention 101
   Chapter Six : Befriending Meditation 113
   Chapter Seven: Befriending Intuition 125
   Chapter Eight: Befriending Creativity 143

PART THREE: SOUL STORY
   Chapter Nine: Listen to Your Life for Your Soul Story 157
   Chapter Ten: The Journey Toward God 175
   Chapter Eleven: The Cobwebbing Power of Destiny Threads 187

Bibliography 205
Book Discussion Guide 207
More Books by Rosalie Deer Heart 211

Dedicated to

Mother Mary

Beings of Light throughout dimensions

Individual Source Codes and the Source Code of our planet

Mother Earth who embodies soul in nature

Our past and future ancestors who are friends of our souls

In Outrageous Appreciation and Deep Bows to:

Alison Strickland, a friend of my soul and extraordinary editor who not only devoted many hours to make this book shine, but also insisted that I include more personal stories and leave research and statistics to others.

Daniel Holeman, a gifted artist and soul friend who created the picture called The Sizzling Heart that became the cover of Soul Befriending.

Megan Don, a spiritual director and woman of my heart who practices love in all ways.

Squidge Davis, a friend of my soul who reminds me to be fully grounded in my body and Being before making my first gesture to clay, stone, and life.

Valerie Kitchen, a friend of my soul and an amazing Pilate's teacher who reminds me to stay in my body's imprint as I strengthen my body and laugh.

Jane and Joe Zenk, who appreciate being grandparents and remind me of the yummy gifts of friendship.

Georgia and Dennis Kosciusko, two lights who blessed my work and me for seven months while we all grew in love and nurtured the land and each other.

Lou Ann Daly a friend of my soul who lights up my life with her wit, wisdom, compassion and trust.

Jean McKillop a friend of my soul, who brings precision, beauty and vision to my website.

Lynn Potoff, a friend of my soul, who grounds me in the third dimensional world and cheers me on in the other realms.

Barbara Cook, a friend of my soul who encourages me to be great and grateful because she is!

Maryann Russell, a friend of my soul, who encourages me to share my love, intuition and stories.

To my PEO sisters worldwide for their kindness, vision, and service that provide millions of dollars in college scholarships and loans to women who will become future leaders.

Introduction

I was born to teach. One of the main themes of my life has been teaching, whether in a classroom, my psychotherapy office, over the phone doing soul readings, writing books or facilitating retreats. Both of my grand children have benefitted from my delight in teaching whether I ask them, "Who is the peace maker here?" or explain how to make piecrust.

I wrote this book to remind you that you have a choice about which story you choose to star in—your limited personal story that is grounded in coping and surviving or your expanded soul story that is centered on transforming, being authentic and embodying spaciousness.

No matter how immersed someone is in their limited personal story, I know a larger soul story co-exists that highlights soul purpose, life lessons, healing potential, creative self expression, and meaningful service. I have enjoyed doing soul readings for more than thirty-five years, which is half of my life! When I was a psychotherapist, I listened for a person's soul purpose and soul agreements because I knew intuitively that was the key to their empowerment, fulfillment and healing.

I am convinced that becoming aware of our individual spiritual perspective is an essential skill. Remembering and reclaiming all of who we are is our evolutionary responsibility. Unfortunately, our culture does not support being awake to our expansive soul story. It saddens me to acknowledge to myself and others that I know many people who continue to align with the drama, trauma, and karma of their personal stories and seem to have amnesia about their co-existing soul story.

The teacher in me relates to this book as a year's workshop between covers.

At the end of each chapter you will find activities, questions for further reflection, and some of my favorite quotations to deepen your awareness and experience of yourself. Readers of my previous book, *Awaken,* encouraged me to include more stories and examples. I have done my best to lead with stories and examples that point to principles and practices.

Writing this book reminded me of playing hopscotch as a little girl. Sometimes I wrote about having one foot in personal story and one foot in soul story. Other times I clearly had both feet in personal story. In the final two chapters I landed with both feet in soul story. However, my journey was not that easy or organized.

My life meandered. Separating the themes into individual chapters was a challenge because ego and soul co-exist and we are in relationship with everything all the time. Only our perspectives are unique. I introduce the subject of past lifetimes, karma, and vows early on because my experience is that we are multi-dimensional Beings and that reality impacts both our personal story and soul story.

I ask a lot of you as a reader. I also asked a lot of myself as I learned how to negotiate the different needs, motivations, and rewards of my personal story and my soul story. Each chapter contains personal stories, principles, examples, dreams, channeling as well as invitations to discover and explore your ongoing story as well as your history.

You will discover many of my journal entries scattered throughout this book. I have been a dedicated journal keeper for half of my lifetime and that has been a profound practice in honesty, radical vulnerability, and expansion of my consciousness. Alison Strickland, one of my evolutionary buddies and editor of this book, and I wrote *Harvesting Your Journals* to encourage people to keep a journal and to use their recorded experiences to cultivate more meaning and direction. I encourage you to keep an ongoing journal as you read.

The first step is awareness. Once we remember how to track our awareness we can appreciate that we are always at a choice point between the two stories. Since life is purposeful, we can then move on and track our motivations and habits of mind and heart that determine which version of our story brings us meaning and fulfillment.

If you are ready to retire from your personal story and nurture your evolving soul story, this book will encourage, challenge and inspire you to live your life on high beam. *Soul Befriending* is an invitation to embody your spiritual legacy as well as your human story. I believe that each of us carries a template or imprint of our soul agreements. We each have specific gifts and talents that only we can embody for the highest good of all. The time is now. We are here. All is ready. Even you!

Like any other journey there are preparations to make, provisions to bring along, people to meet and love, and places to go. I recommend you pack the following essentials to accompany you on the journey:

- Open heart and an open mind
- Compassion for self and others
- Curiosity
- Optimism
- A Sense of Humor
- A mirror to reflect your essence
- Chocolate for letting go and celebration
- A journal to record connections, questions, insights, and dreams

I chose to embrace my evolving soul story because I do not know how many breaths I will get this lifetime. As a teacher and cosmic catalyst, I also challenge others as well as myself to respond to this question: "If you were taking your last breaths at this moment, what would you desire to remember and what would you regret?" Then I take a deep, conscious breath and remind us that it is not too late to make definitive choices and deep changes that align us with our expansive soul story. Several years ago I adopted Stephen Levine's advice: "If you had an hour to live and could make only one phone call, who would you call, what would you say and why are you waiting?"

Leave your GPS behind. Growth happens at the intersections between what we don't know and what we are willing to encounter. Be prepared to question all of your beliefs, especially the ones you cherish the most deeply. When you align with your soul, you may discover delight. Be open to possibilities and synchronicities. Act as if you are already neck deep in grace. You may experience time differently. It may appear to be more fluid and present time may blend and merge with past time or flow into future time. Your guides may invite you to play and transform guidance into wisdom. God may seize you.

Along the way expect to:

- grow in self confidence and spiritual confidence
- trade in a personal story for soul story
- befriend your emotions, especially judged or buried feelings
- break rank with ways you dim your light
- look for the joy potential in every opportunity
- reclaim talents that add to your wholeness and sense of well-being

Count on me as your travel guide to remind you to love yourself, your life, and all that you attract. Both love and compassion carry a higher frequency than fear, blame, guilt and shame. Love without exceptions. Love is the radiant, transformative energy that connects us with all that is. Join me in adopting an evolutionary affirmation: I am love loving. Enjoy being open to how your life transforms.

As you read the following pages and chapters, my special prayer is that your soul spark ignites and fires your cosmic memory and you remember your spaciousness, which is your light legacy, as well as your unique soul purpose. Then allow yourself to be open to a sacred truth: You are the person you have been waiting for! In the words of Big Angel, one of my recent guides who you will meet in this book, *"Fully flourishing is one of the pleasures that you can claim in your humanness. You each have the capacity to fully flourish. Be aware of what inspires you, renews you, and makes you feel irresistible. That is your inheritance and your legacy."*

The earth awaits. Evolution awaits.

If you are ready to experience your own evolutionary transformation and add to the expanded consciousness of our world and planet, welcome to your ever evolving, co-creative story.

Section One

The Power of Stories

Chapter One

Personal Story or Soul Story: Your Choice

"Everything is held together by stories. That is all that is holding us together, stories and compassion."

Barry Lopez

I grew up outside of Portland, Maine where there was a twin drive-in movie theater where it was possible to park in a specific aisle and view both movies simultaneously. I loved the challenge of being dual focused! Since I believe that we are all spiritual beings who have lived many life times and we are here to learn about the human experience, I believe that we are capable of running two stories simultaneously—our contracted personal story and our expansive soul story.

The journey from being claimed by personal story to being aligned with soul story is about moving out of unconsciousness and into consciousness. Yesterday I sat with a woman who was despondent about her life. Her husband left their thirty-year marriage for another woman and six years later she continued to feel his departure as a soul betrayal. She resented living alone because she was raised to believe that despite life's "ups and downs," married people remained loyal to one another. She had distanced herself from her friends, feeling like a burden because she had nothing to give back. When her employer reduced her full time job to twelve hours a week, she hit bottom. She complained that she had no energy to look for another job and she was too old to begin another career. Grief and suppressed anger were audible in both her words and her sighs. No partner, no friends she could confide in, no job security, and no energy.

Although I felt compassion for her, I was struck by how perfectly she had created the events that brought her to this threshold between personal story and soul story. I know from experience that a threshold offers you a unique opportunity to be aware of your hopes and resources as well as your self-sabotaging strategies. The transition is from leading a life that is ego directed to a life that is soul centered. She was at a choice point—either immerse herself in self-pity and resign herself to being a victim of her personal story or challenge her beliefs, take responsibility for what she had created in her life and move forward into the future and her soul story.

I took a deep breath to center myself and congratulated her on her genius because I was aware how she had created her own tipping point. Whether she would choose to sabotage herself or move forward was her choice. Then I asked her to consider how where she was in her life was perfect. She looked puzzled. When she got up and moved out of her chair and stood in front of me, I did not know if she planned to hit me or hug me. Then she laughed and I knew she had broken through the fear and inertia of her personal story. Be aware! The greater the transformational risk, the more your ego will react to try to control and to sabotage you.

Later the same night I returned to re-reading Carlos Castaneda's *The Eagle's Gift*. In it he tells the story of his struggles to remember who he was and claim his gifts. Again I was struck by the power of the many obstacles that he created and confronted in order to align with his soul story.

Move ahead nine hours. I am sitting in my meditation loft with my friend Georgia. During our daily morning meditation, I reflected on how blessed I feel and how easy my life feels now. Embracing my soul story creates a flow in my life. Joy is a daily companion. Laughter feels as natural as my breath.

That was when I thought about Andrea, the woman whom I sat with yesterday and Carlos and his struggle to remember himself. With stunning clarity I revisited times in my life when I was under the light-dimming spell of my personal story. My body remembers the specifics of many painful encounters—deaths, disease, divorces, depression, bankruptcy, voluntary exile, and other dramatic events. Eventually I made conscious choices to move beyond my personal story. I lost innocence and gained experience, clarity, boundaries, and wisdom. Looking back I can now see it all unfolded perfectly. Even I was perfect.

I believe that each of us was born magnificent and as we grew up, we dimmed our light and settled for mediocrity. Together we can end the trance of our learned limitations and personal history and choose to align with our expanded soul story. Remember your soul story is forever your context even when your personal story appears to be the one you are more comfortable starring in and repeating to others. The questions to ask yourself to determine whether you are engaging in your personal story or your soul story are always the same:

- What do I see?
- How deeply do I allow myself to see?
- What don't I see?
- Where is the presence of love?

When I am the most honest and the most vulnerable, I know that I agreed to be an apprentice of love this lifetime. I have been practicing love forever. (Some people might say that I am a slow learner.) The theme of my last book, *Awaken,* was an invitation to open our hearts to love.

Since I have been a dedicated journal keeper for more than four decades, I can track my apprenticeship to love. In retrospect, I realize that if I had lived my life in alignment with the following principles that I wrote in 1996 during a women's writer's conference at Skidmore College, I would be in daily alignment with my soul story. The "She" I refer to is my Guide or Muse.

She always told me to listen, especially at night when the house was quiet.
She always told me that truth lives in my body.
She always told me to trust her goodwill as well as my own.
She always told me she was available to comfort me, guide me, and inspire me if I remembered to call her.
She always told me to honor my origins as well as my future.
She always told me that I create the future out of the past and I am the only one in charge of determining my future.
She always told me to trust in the power of love to heal and that it is love that creates intimacy and then expands to infinity.
She always told me that I was a blessing and that my life mattered.

She always told me to celebrate the little girl who lived within my heart and to include her in each decision I made.

She always told me that love was eternal and each time I chose to love I added to the consciousness of light regardless of the consequences of loving.

She always told me to create a place for silence each day.

She always told me to appreciate the ever-expanding spiral of the sacred amidst the daily events of my life.

She always told me to keep my heart open and invite my soul to collaborate and remind me of the deeper meanings of love and life. And I believed her.

The Power of Stories

Here's a story that illustrates how alive you can become when you attune to your soul story:

Sitting in the reception room, waiting for my favorite healer-dentist, Pam Anzelac, I locked eyes with a little girl who looked about five years old. We smiled. She got off the couch where she was sitting with her mother and little brother, sat down in the chair next to me and began talking as if we were old friends. I was delighted to entertain her and she sensed my invitation.

"You know what I saw yesterday at my camp—a big, fat red cardinal? I laid down quietly on my belly in the grass so I wouldn't scare the bird and guess what?"

Without waiting for a response from me, she continued, "He sang to me. A song I never heard before."

"How sweet," I said returning her smile.

"Then you know what I did?" she said eagerly.

"Tell me," I said with excitement.

"I sang a little girl's song to the cardinal. A different song than the ones I sing to robins and blackbirds. I have never made up a cardinal song before. It was fun."

"How did you find the cardinal song?" I asked.

"I listened in my heart," she said matter of factly.

"And then what did your bird friend do?" I asked.

"He turned his head to listen to the beginning of my song to him and then he hopped away."

I thanked her for sharing her story and told her I would remember her and her story every time I spotted a cardinal.

She shook her head and said, "That's not enough. Since I told you my story, you have to lay down in the grass and sing an old lady's cardinal song."

I laughed, and said, "It's a deal."

Her mother barked, "Eliza, it's not okay to call someone an old lady."

Eliza looked surprised and in no way looked like she planned to apologize.

I looked at her mother and said, "I am sure I am an old lady to her. It's okay with me. She was speaking her truth."

Eliza smiled and gave me a high five.

Each time that I remember her and her cardinal story, I smile. She naturally tunes into her intuition, tells her truth, and shares her magic with anyone who appears to have an open heart. She is my kind of person!

Who Are You?

Who we are is deeply connected to what stories we tell and repeat about others, the world and ourselves. The narratives we tell are the stories we live. Soul story and personal story have different frequencies, needs, and capacities. Ego is the place of control and dimming our light. Personality, which is an aspect of soul, is the self that we present to the world. Many of us navigate our life based solely on our ego's personal story.

When I visited my friend Alice in her new home, I was impressed with the spaciousness of her large art room. It was the largest and lightest room in her home. Every inch of space was covered with clay, brushes, paints and sculpting tools. A large, expensive kiln still wrapped in layers of Styrofoam and not hooked up set in the backyard. I was puzzled.

"How long has the kiln been outside?" I asked.

"About two years," she replied. "I still haven't figured out a way to hook it up."

I was aware I did not want to listen to her excuses, which I could predict from past history—not enough time, too much other work to do, an absence of teachers, the lack of support from a partner, and no money.

When her partner returned home, she immediately confronted him with the question, "How come you don't play your guitar and create music like you used to?"

Not surprisingly, his excuses echoed hers.

I congratulated her for asking an important question. Then I encouraged each of them to make space in their daily lives for their unique forms of creative expression. Breaking through rigid beliefs is ongoing work. When we have inner and outer support for trance ending, maintaining the commitment is easier. Remember the ego contracts. It fears the unknown and is resistant to change. One of its jobs is to preserve the status quo. If the status quo is inertia, the ego will resist efforts to grow.

We were all trained to fulfill the expectations of others. It takes awareness, will, commitment and daily practice to deconstruct ingrained patterns of codependence. However there is good news! Enlightened awareness, which is grounded in your soul story, is the capacity to be free from history and time. Soul is the place of expansiveness and joyful service.

The Twists and Turns of Ego

Our personal story is grounded on what is important to our ego and ego does not discern between needs. As adults we know that not every need is valid. Ego is like a child who wants what it wants now and it is seldom satisfied. For example, if my ego is running the show and I spot a chocolate cake on the counter, I go for it, without even checking to see if I am hungry. My impulsive ego does not care to question about the source of my emptiness.

Ego, which runs our personal story, tends to be loud, habitual, and afraid. Like a spoiled child, it demands what it wants and it is never satisfied. It thrives on drama. As a general rule, when you feel afraid, upset, angry, judgmental, hurt or embarrassed, your ego is at work. Each time you react from the edges of your personality you invite defensiveness from others. If you do not disengage from your ego, it will dominate and block out soul.

This journal entry exposes my exploding ego:

"I'm not good enough" broke through my growing relationship with clay today. It began when I questioned myself about my dedication to making more rattles. I almost sabotaged myself by questioning if my motivation to create more rattles was a trick to avoid working on the pottery wheel because I am afraid I am not creative enough. Then I lost my balance and my ego screamed, "You are not enough. You are not creative enough, smart enough, strong enough, patient enough, compassionate enough, giving enough, or coordinated enough." My shoulders drooped, my breathing slowed down, and I felt shamed, silent and young.

I breathed, determined to track when this life sucking voice began. I stalked the light diminishing voice as it echoed through decades of my life. I judged myself as not a good enough student, dancer, daughter, friend, lover and partner. Each time I believed my ego's tyrannical voice, I noticed that I moved further away from my heart, my voice and my confidence.

Arguing or defending myself did not appease my hungry ego. Giving in to my old program of shutting down my creativity was no longer an option.

Breathing, and allowing myself to sink deeper into the habitual, bullying voice seemed like the most direct approach. Squidge Davis, my pottery teacher, encouraged me to allow this toxic belief to pierce me like an arrow by sitting with it, feeling it, getting to know it and then grieving it. We both agreed that unless I felt fully into my core wound, I had no way to heal it.

I walked to Grandfather tree instinctively knowing I was safe there. Next I dropped to my knees and dug a deep hole. Then I screamed my pain and shame into the dark earth. Eventually I cried. After a long time I invited my inner little girl back into my life. She hesitated at first. Then I surrounded her with love and invited her again. She arrived with dirty, bruised knees, a fascination for worms, an instinctual dislike for phony people, an adventurous spirit, laughter, a sense of rhythm and symmetry, and jokes and riddles that made no sense.

"You are so much more than enough" I crooned to her.

Compassion threatens the ego. Failure and rejection are tricks of the ego and the names we give to feeling disempowered.

Later I wrote:

I am alive.
I am dynamic.
I am creative.
I am light.

I celebrate life.
I celebrate Nature.
I celebrate playfulness.
I celebrate coincidences and miracles.
I celebrate God and raspberries.

Think of ego as core resistance to soul. Some people call ego the false self and soul the true self. Dimming our light and our potential by playing small and safe, or feeling victimized are other ego strategies as well as gossiping and comparing ourselves to others. Ego twists truth. I know I am starring in my personal story when I catch myself acting defensively or engaging in uproar. Other signals that I am immersed in the quicksand of my ego include making excuses and not being honest with others and myself.

When we drop into ego, we become scared, judgmental and limited. The way to break bonds with limiting beliefs is to align with the energy of your soul. Love and a sense of unlimited possibilities resonate with soul. My inner little girl has a soul perspective.

The Pull of Personal Story

Every thought and action we embody resonates with our small personal story or our expansive soul story. Focus on what you are aware of in order to be present for what is happening moment to moment. Then expand your awareness to identify what's keeping you confined to your personal story. These questions will help you clarify your personal story.

- Who are the main characters and the supporting cast in your personal story?
- What are your strongest limiting beliefs that fuel your personal story?
- What are the themes of your most repeated personal stories?
- What keeps you connected to your personal story?
- What does your personal story offer you?
- What does your personal story ask of you?

Here's a personal story that one woman created:

"I am surrounded by wicked people," a woman who I had never seen before complained as we waited for a chiropractic appointment.

Without thinking, I said, "Tell them to all go away."

"I do. And they keep coming back."

"Then you go away," I said calmly looking her directly in the eyes.

She sighed. I smiled and let go of more words and any expectations.

"You don't understand. The only time I feel in touch with my strong energy is when I head butt with the wicked people in my life."

I breathed and let myself feel how my life would feel if I harbored her belief.

Then I said, "Imagine how much energy you would have for yourself if you fired yourself from attracting wicked people into your life."

I believe that nothing outside attacks us. I know from experience that we are only assaulted by our own thoughts, needs, and attachments and they are all connected to small self and ego.

If you are feeling gypped by others or life, your ego is in control. Identify with the witness instead of ego. True self is often called witness. The witness is the place of deep awareness, non-attachment, and fresh insight. It is also called mirror mind because it reflects everything that arises, but does not grasp or get attached. It is the place inside of your consciousness where you can watch the whole drama unfolding without becoming attached to the story or its outcome. (You will learn about how to align with your inner witness in Chapter Six.)

Perspectives Are Personal

Here's a situation where four different people react to the same incident and connect with their personal story or their soul story. Remember it is what you see and what you don't see that determines your perspectives and hence the story you are living into.

I woke up to the early morning sound of my daughter's screams from her bedroom upstairs. I rushed up the stairs and into her bedroom. She was standing at the top of her bed shrieking with her right arm pointing to a mound of blankets in the middle of her bed.

Noah and Malia stood beside the bed. Their faces looked concerned and serious but not scared.

"Look, mice, dead mice under the blankets in the middle of my bed. Ugh!"

She must have thrown the covers over their dead bodies.

When I pulled the covers off, Malia, Noah and I moved closer to look.

"Do you think they suffered?" asked Malia, reaching her hand out to touch them.

Noah shook his head and asked me, "How much do you think the soul of a mouse weighs, Grandmom?"

I watched all of us as if we were in a movie. I was aware of our individual perspectives and reactions to the same event and I even wondered about Wizard, the hunter-mother cat's perspective. Whether our reaction is dramatic or curious or objective determines if we're running our personal story or our soul story.

Here is another story that helps me understand how ego can disguise itself as inner guidance and distort perception. As it unfolded, as long as I kept a witness perspective I was not pulled into another's personal story.

I journeyed to Giant Rock outside Palm Springs, Ca. with friends to experience the quartz mound. When we arrived at the top, I felt strange, like raindrops were falling on my head but that was impossible because the sun was bright. Then I noticed my heart was beating faster than normal. When my eyes seemed to close on their own accord, I recognized the familiar signals that I associate with channeling.

I opened my mouth and the transmission continued for more than an hour. The energies felt unfamiliar yet friendly to me. When I inquired who was responsible for downloading the information, I was told, "Extra-Terrestrials or E.T.'s, who now wish to be known as Stellans, which means "from the stars." I was conscious of the information coming through me as I channeled and I enjoyed the uplifting frequency.

Several months later one of the friends who accompanied me to Giant Rock insisted that he was ready to channel the Stellans. I was surprised and said I did not think we were in charge of deciding when we were ready to channel other energies much less command their presence. He disagreed saying, "I know I am ready. I know it is time and I will command the stellar energies to flow through me. And I would like you to come."

Then he loaded his sleeping bag, water, and a few candy bars into the car and we headed to Giant Rock, outside of Joshua Tree, Ca. During the three-hour drive, I let go of my perspective and feelings and reminded myself that this was not my movie. I planned to watch the stars dot the night sky and then return to a nearby motel. My friend was prepared to camp out the whole night and as many days and nights as it took.

We arrived at the designated place a few minutes before sunset. The sun was setting and a full moon also lit the sky. I spread out a blanket and watched the changing landscape while he buried an offering in the sand and snuggled up in his sleeping bag. I continued to sit as the stars appeared. Then I got cold and hungry. I wished my friend good luck and carefully walked down the quartz mound.

A few hours later, he returned to the motel. I didn't need to be intuitive to know that the Stellans had not responded to his command. Yet I did not need to revel in being right. He was silent. I choose to be silent too because I knew if I spoke, I would enter his personal story.

Ram Dass puts it this way, "Learn to watch your drama unfold while at the same time knowing you are more than your drama."

The Stories Continue

Your ego does not like to admit that you may be filled with denial, conflict, mixed emotions, shame, guilt, and other confusing emotions. Here is a story of an epic ego struggle that endured beyond this lifetime.

I was called into the hospital to consult with an elderly man, named Matthew, because his physician was unable to come up with a clear diagnosis.

He feared Matthew would suffer a stroke or heart attack because the medications were not working. I do not look at the hospital charts or listen to the person's case history before meeting with the patient. I want to be a clear channel.

Matthew agreed to see me alone at the hospital because he was curious about the energy work I do. When we shook hands, he said, "So you will read my energy and then what?"

I shrugged my shoulders and said frankly, "I have no idea. We will have to see what unfolds. I am not in charge of the information or your choices."

"Good," he said with a slight laugh, "everyone else in this hospital acts as if they know everything and nobody seems get it straight about what's wrong with me."

I explained that in my work energy is simply information and I would ask his guides for information about his health, with his permission.

"Go for it," he said and winked at me.

I merged with his energy and then called in his guides and asked them to give me information about his physical condition.

Immediately, I sensed the presence of another energy in his energy field. It felt like feminine energy. Before I sent out gratitude for incoming information, I heard a voice say, "Tell him Edith demands to talk to him."

I said to Matthew, "Tell me about Edith."

He gasped and turned pale. Then he said, "You mean my ex-wife?"

"I will check," I replied.

When I returned to the energy that I felt as Edith, I inquired, "Are you Matthew's ex-wife?"

"I am his wife," she said somewhat petulantly. "I hate that he calls me his ex-wife. We never divorced. We were married for 68 years. I am not his ex-anything. Tell him he cannot discard me so easily. I will see to that."

Her voice sounded threatening and I could feel her hurt and anger.

Then I disconnected from the energy of Edith and returned to speak to Matthew.

"Matthew, I said, "Would you consider not calling Edith your ex-wife?"

"Hell, no," he said loudly. "Not after two years of her keeping me awake at night and harping on that. Sometimes it feels like she is putting pressure on my heart and lungs. And I am not imagining this," he said with emphasis.

"Have you told your doctor about your problems not being able to sleep at night?"

"Are you kidding? They would throw me in the psychiatric ward if I told them how she taunts me. And then she would win for sure. She is the cause of my suffering and pain. I knew it."

"Matthew, is it okay with you if I ask your wife, Edith what she needs in order to leave your energy field and resume her own journey?"

"That depends. Does she know she is dead and we are not married anymore?"

"Matthew, I believe she knows she is dead and she also knows you are not dead. However, I suspect you hold different opinions about if you are still married."

"Okay, you can ask her what she needs but that doesn't mean I will give in. She can no longer control me since she is my ex-wife."

I was silent. Although I felt the stalemate that existed between them, I also felt compassion for each of them. I knew that if I got sidetracked by their emotions, I might not be able to access more information.

Once again I moved my energy to connect with Edith's etheric heart and told her I was interested in helping her husband sort out his health issues.

Once again she insisted she was not his ex-wife. "I put up with him for 68 eight years. I will not allow him to dismiss me."

Energetically I acknowledged her anger.

"Damn right, I am angry. And I have made him pay attention, but he won't budge. He has almost died twice."

I asked her if she enjoyed seeing him suffer. Silence. I thought perhaps we had lost contact or she had gotten mad at me, too.

"Edith, if you tell me what you need from Matthew, I will communicate with him and maybe the two of you can heal this painful impasse and go on with your individual journeys."

"I will stop pestering him if he stops calling me his ex-wife," she said. "But don't hold your breath, Dearie, he is one old, stubborn geezer."

I thanked her for sharing and said nothing more.

Matthew looked apprehensive when I again looked him in the eyes. "Your wife said she will leave you alone at night if you stop referring to her as "your ex-wife."

"Never gonna happen," he said loudly. "I am the one who survived and I can call her anything I damn well please."

"Yes, of course you can. But is it worth the price you are paying? This is your fourth hospital stay in five months."

"You don't get it. I am in charge of my life after sixty-eight years of her never listening to me. Yes, I am in pain and I would like to know what is wrong with me, but I will never give in to her."

I made one last effort to broker a truce. Then I remembered one of the most valuable lessons I learned in studying therapy. When I am working harder than my client, it is my issue to deal with. I had done my job, gathered information and the end of the story was up to them.

I thanked both of them and sent love to each one and then disconnected from their energy fields, shook Matthew's hand and left. On the way to my car I reminded myself to breath consciously and invited my breath to help me ground myself in my own energy field. That was when I felt the power of grudges and imagined that Matthew and Edith had created lots of karma this life time and I hoped they would be kinder to one another the next time around.

I wished they could listen to me and I would tell them that one way to avoid power struggles is to ask, "What is being asked of me relative to the organizing principles of my soul?" Or even better, remember this—while in the midst of an ego-driven tug of war, drop your end of the rope. Even more to the point—consider that every place you have blocked out love, a potential miracle did not occur.

Fear or Faith?

Both positive and negative thoughts affect our health and the impact we have on others. Successful manifestation or self-sabotage can be traced directly to our beliefs. If you believe something strongly, you will see evidence of your beliefs everywhere because your beliefs create your reality.

Malia, my twelve-year-old granddaughter, has a difficult time trusting that life is fair. She worries and wants guarantees that life is safe. On the other hand, I tend to trust people and life.

This conversation illustrates how our perspective influences the story we are in the middle of living.

Malia tugged at my arm and said seriously, "Grandmom, I worry about you sometime."

I replied, "I'm sorry."

"What I mean is you trust people too much and too soon and not all people are good, you know."

"You are right, Malia, I trust people and life, too."

"Right Grandmom and sometimes you get hurt."

"That is true and I prefer to have an open heart rather than a closed heart."

"But people can hurt you then."

"Yes, and people can also love me."

"So I have a question for you and I know already just what you will say."

"Okay, let's see if you are right."

" If when you went home today, you found your front door broken open and all of your stuff was gone, what would you think?"

"Well, first of all, I don't lock my door. Second I would be surprised and then I would remember it is only stuff—not like a person's life—and I can replace stuff if I choose. If my heart was really open I might think that the robber needed the stuff more than me."

"I knew you would say all those things, Grandmom. That is why I worry about you."

"You know, Malia there is an old Sufi song about a robber who broke into a man's house and the song goes, "He took everything except love."

She shook her head and sighed. I smiled. I wished I had remembered to share one of my favorite John O'Dea quotations from his book *Creative Stress*. "We possess only that which survives a shipwreck." What I know from my experience is that unless we change our perspective, we will attract what we expect to manifest.

Here are a few personal stories to help you to gain a deeper appreciation and understanding of the pain and suffering that we generate when we attach to our limited, ego driven narratives.

The repetitive theme of Abby's personal story was being pursued by evil energies that were determined to take over her body, steal her light, and prevent her from becoming an artist. She spent hours each day clearing her energy field and crafting strategies to insure that the dark energies would not return. She spoke of her demons as her "visitors." Even when she succeeded in banishing them she said confidently, "Now I must prepare myself for an all out battle because they will regroup and come after me full force."

The visitors have her in their control because she is fully focused on them instead of her own light and potential. Remember that beliefs can move us forward or hold us back. Negative thinking is an addiction that drains energy.

Max's soul purpose was to embody personal vision. Yet the story he told me centered on how he exhausted himself by supporting everyone else's vision. Even when I interrupted his story to remind him of his soul purpose, which is his evolutionary obligation, he engaged in "Yes, but." Without taking a breath, he sabotaged himself asking, "What if my family does not support my vision?" Before I can answer, he asks, "Don't you think I am being selfish by wanting what I want without considering others?" Inertia is evidence of ego.

Here is a collection of compressed true stories that serve as examples of the power of personal stories and suggestions about how to shift into soul story drawn from my soul coaching practice. Until you take 100% responsibility for attracting drama, pain and suffering, you remain hostage to your personal story.

Paul's story: "I want Mary to love me now. I have promised her everything. I refuse to wait for her to make a decision even one day longer."

Paul's ego had a certain model of how things should be and stays closed to any event that does not fit into the narrow circle of his expectations.

Soul allows and heals. When Paul was able to appreciate that Mary gave him a gift of looking at his own need for control, he decided he was ready to learn how to love himself.

Frank's story: "I ripped my knee because I was not looking where I was going and I was over tired and in a rush. What a stupid thing to do! Then I dislocated my shoulder and had an adverse reaction to the medication and then…"

Ego identifies with body and mind. Soul is on the lookout for "What is the gift?" When Frank recognized how he was the source of his grievances and his motivation was to get attention, he agreed to use his creativity to attract people's good will.

Beth's story: "I get hooked by unhappy people or people I see in pain. I want them to feel the love I feel so I make friends with them. Then I am surprised and devastated when they turn against me."

Ego attaches to a person or an outcome. Soul is connected to fuller expansion. When Beth connected to her own pain, she no longer had to attract people she considered unfortunate and learned how to extend love to herself.

Sheila's story: "I am a klutz." In one hour Sheila fell in the mud, forgot her purse, and got lost. With each breath and step she put into action what she believed to be true about herself.

Ego is the voice of limitation. Soul is the place of unlimited possibilities. By taking responsibility for her pattern of not being aware or her lack of focus, Sheila gradually slowed down and no longer branded herself "a klutz."

Jo's story: "I always seem to just get by financially. I always seem to have just enough—nothing more— to get by each month. I work harder and harder every month and the result is the same."

Anxiety comes from the ego's need to protect itself. "Always" and "Never" indicate that ego is running the show.

Soul is the place of abundance and wellbeing. When Jo connected her financial struggles with her father's story of bankruptcy and suicide, she was shocked. Unwilling to continue to be loyal to her father's personal story, she empowered herself by taking a well paying job out of state and returning to college to get her Master's Degree in Counseling.

Inertia or Evolution?

We change when we change our consciousness. Morris Massey's research proved that few people make significant life changes after the age of 13. Core values and strategies are locked in and rarely change unless the person experiences a significant emotional event. Mark Gafni, in his book *Unique Self* cites further research that says that the majority of people stop growing at age twenty-six. This is disturbing news for those of us who wish to grow beyond our personal story. In order to move beyond the inertia that is too often created by unquestioned allegiance to our personal story, we need evolutionary buddies in our life. While friends may love you and encourage you to be your best, evolutionary buddies will challenge you and act as your spiritual mirrors. They will demand that you live your life full beam and will not be seduced with who you used to be in the past. In fact, evolutionary buddies are more connected to who you are capable of becoming in the future than who you have been in the past.

The Principle of Co-Arising

You can expect backlash in the psyche that bubbles up as fear, anxiety, or clinging to the familiar after a breakthrough. The principle of co-arising frequently appears after we challenge our survival instinct that is rooted around protection and self-preservation. For example, if I make an intention to meditate every day, I can expect myself to find ways to forget, make excuses or avoid meditating.

When I teach, I remind people that if they are making a commitment to practice self-love, they will probably trip over self-judgment or whatever they consider the polarity of love.

Let go of making the backlash attack mean anything. In other words, notice its strategy and move on. Like guests who have over stayed their welcome, if you don't feed them, they leave. Please be aware that there is always a part of us that wants no part of revelation because it separates us from our history.

The Many Facets of Ego

Ego thrives on creating distance and a sense of separation. It does its best to eclipse soul. Another place to look for ego traces is any place in your life where you defend yourself and cause suffering to yourself and others. Stalk patterns of self-neglect, which, if not challenged, lead to self-abandonment. Self-pity, which takes a lot of energy to maintain, is another ego trap. People who are invested in playing the Poor Me or The Sorry game are addicted to the victim role. They trap themselves with their thinking, forgetting that they have the power to change their thinking and often their circumstances. Complaints and sighs replace action.

When you feel or observe any of these elements in yourself or someone else, you can be sure ego is in control.

- Fear Centered
- Self Abandonment
- Drama
- Shame
- Struggle and Suffering
- Maintaining status quo through control

- Defensiveness
- Blaming others
- Over functioning or under functioning
- Pessimism
- Polarized thinking and behaving that results in inner and outer splits
- Denial of personal and collective shadow
- Avoidance of uncertainty and the unknown

Unraveling The Layers

Let's begin at the beginning. Our core identity is intimately connected to our early role in our family. We learned our survival strategies, how to feel, how to relate to others, how to please, how to think, how to succeed, as well as how to sabotage ourselves in our family circle. Our family's beliefs are deeply wired within us. In our family of origin we learned to play the role of the adapted self. Think of this role as our pleaser self. For years I pretended to enjoy listening to the Red Sox on the radio because my father was a big fan. Sometimes we forget that it is a role and we live out our life from our adapted self-perspective until we receive a wake up call to make room for our authentic self.

~Take a breath and make a commitment to be radically honest as you respond to the following questions:

- In what ways do you continue to relate to yourself that replicate the ways your parents treated you?
- What are your family's favorite stories about you?
- How would your life be different if you made conscious choices in place of unexamined ancestral beliefs?
- What is the cost of going against family rules and beliefs?
- Whose stories do you get caught in?
- How magnificent can you be and continue to be embraced by your family of origin?
- When or where do you avoid being who you truly are?

Granted, some people inherited healthy beliefs and behaviors from their families. If you are one of the fortunate few, please honor and celebrate your positive legacy and make a commitment to play it forward.

Breaking Rank

As a fifth generation woman from Maine, I was trained to serve others, defer my needs until there was spare time, swallow my emotions, and deny my authentic self. Intergenerational family rules included: Be strong. Work hard. Take care of the needs of others. Respect your elders and do not question. Be loyal to family—no matter what. For years I sourced my value by being a strange combination of the wacky Gracie Allen and the self sacrificing Florence Nightingale. I longed for acceptance and love.

If you value social acceptance and approval from others as more essential to your life than your authentic self-expression, you are caught in your personal story. When my spiritual advisor challenged me by asking, "Rosie, hasn't anyone every told you did not come here for acceptance?" I knew she was right. I also acknowledged that I had devoted many years to dimming my light and my expression in order to belong to groups and my family. My body felt lighter as I breathed in the larger truth. I felt free to be me. Knowing that I no longer needed to win a popularity contest created a bridge to live more fully into my soul story.

Breaking rank with your personal history means challenging all of your personal and inherited beliefs and letting go of learned limitations that resonate with: I'm not enough, I am unlovable, I do not deserve, I am too much, or I don't have what it takes to realize my dreams.

It is essential to identify our inherited, unconscious belief patterns because they have a negative impact. When you suspect that your ego is running the show, consider these questions.

- What belief is sustaining or undermining my action?
- Is this belief true for me?
- What do I gain by this belief?
- Who would I be without this belief?
- Is this belief expansive or contractive?
- What would I have to give up or do to change this light dimming belief?

Personal Story or Soul Story: Your Choice

When you look inside yourself, you will find that there are many competing personalities. There are the traditional roles we identify with which might include: child, parent, brother, sister, partner, friend, male, female as well as the work we do. Also, we all house sub-personalities such as clown, victim, rescuer, lover, hero, rock star or dreamer. It is not difficult to imagine that conflict could arise within the many ego roles we play.

When we stop responding to our ego's need for power and control, it loses some of its power. One of the ways to move out of the influence of our ego is to ask: What am I responsible for? Offering help to someone in need is different from taking responsibility for his or her wellbeing. As a woman I have created thousands of opportunities to remind myself to take a breath, move into my high heart, and ask if I have a soul responsibility for this particular person before agreeing to be a lifeline.

This story demonstrates how I was pushed to listen to my soul in the midst of a tragic situation. In July 2012, I committed to a four-week residential artist's retreat. I had never dreamed of giving myself such a gift. Talk about creative generosity! I felt both scared and in touch with a sense of the sacred in the weeks and days before I embarked on my journey.

I would have no access to newspapers, Internet, television, or other electronics. Eight days into my mostly silent artist's retreat, my childhood friend Darlena tracked me down to tell me that she was dying. The aggressive cancer that had been decimated during radiation returned and was galloping throughout her debilitated body.

She was scared. She was an only child and both her parents were dead. We had been friends for sixty years with a few years out because of misunderstandings. She wanted me with her. She knew I had served as a midwife to people who had cradled death. Although she acted optimistic when we had a pajama party a few weeks earlier, I left knowing she was dying.

I have a reputation for being a loyal and responsible woman. Like many women, I also have a history of over-giving and over-achieving. Compassion fatigue has claimed me more times than I care to count this lifetime. Grounded in my heart as well as my body and surrounded by ancient trees and a clear, starry sky, I asked: What is my spiritual responsibility to myself and to Darlena? Then I asked: What is the right action here?

My heart's response was instant. My guidance was to remain on retreat for the next twenty-two days. As I continued to breathe into my heart's truth, I acknowledged that I knew how to energetically support Darlena long distance. I also knew she had other friends who would support her until I arrived in three weeks. I also prayed for her to regain her clarity about how she wished to die. I prayed for a merciful and peaceful death.

Sometimes choices are hard. I struggled with being selfish and then reminded myself that energetic support counts. I called her and offered to be with her full time in three weeks. I am proud to write after much work and practice, I now know I am entitled to feel joyful even when others are in pain.

I often refer back to this quotation by Hazrat Pir-o-Murshid Inayat Khan when I need validation for putting my soul needs first: "Once you have given up your limited self willingly to the Unlimited, you will rejoice so much in that consciousness that you will not care to be small again."

The Basics: Breath and Body

Let's return to the basics—your body and your breath. I often remind myself to detach from my brain and return to my breath. Breath keeps everything moving. Lack of movement in your body means you are not breathing into those places that are blocked. Close your eyes and focus on your breathing. Experience your breath just as it is moment to moment without judging or trying to change it.

Be aware of how you inhale and receive air and how you exhale and release air. Stay connected to your breathing long enough to be aware of the rhythm of your inhale and exhale.

- Which is longer—the inhale or the exhale?
- Are you breathing from your mouth or your nose?
- Is your breath coming from the top of your chest or the bottom of your belly?
- Is your breath flowing, tight, shallow, or rapid?

Think about your body as your subconscious mind. When we remember how to think through our body, our ego forfeits some of its domination. When I make a conscious decision to honor my body, I am often surprised how it responds to my kindness and keeps me strong and healthy. Often I am surprised as ideas and connections pop up when I am walking my four cats or bending over while I weed the vegetable garden.

I remember learning to ice skate when I was about seven years old. My favorite part, aside from the hot chocolate, was gliding after many steps of pushing my skates forward to gain momentum. The glide felt like a free ride and made all the effort worthwhile. I can still remember the feeling of freedom in my body, which now feels a bit like grace, and I return to my body memory of gliding when I find myself struggling with a problem.

I have a long-standing habit of neglecting my body and its rhythms and needs. Growing up, I do not remember either my grandmother or my mother exercising or enjoying outdoor activities. For recreation my mother knitted and my grandmother sewed. Outdoor sports were for boys. I, too, adopted a sedentary lifestyle. When I was thirty-two years old, I had an unwanted emergency hysterectomy. Then I decided I could no longer neglect my body. After I had recovered from the surgery, I enrolled in exercise classes to regain my strength and to keep my weigh under control. Hot flashes were another assault. Since I was a feminist, I was convinced I could control hot flashes. Wrong! Even though I did my best to re-frame hot flashes as power surges, the result was the same. I could not trust my body to be normal.

However, I marched myself to exercise classes three times a week for a couple of years and then stopped abruptly. I took up cross-country skiing in the winter and hiking during the three other seasons.

When I turned sixty, I went in for a routine physical and the doctor threatened to put me in the hospital because my blood pressure was so high. I chose exercise and meditation over medication. The threat of a stroke motivated me to show up at Curves three days a week. I also added a two-mile walk three days a week to my exercise routine. I was determined to take control of my health and bought a portable blood pressure cuff and monitored my blood pressure. Within two months my blood pressure had returned to normal.

After a couple of years, I got bored with Curves and committed myself to a rigorous swimming routine three days a week. While swimming laps, I had conversations in my head and played with my imagination. The problem was I had to drive thirty minutes to get to the pool, undress, shower, and dress again. After several months, my skin began to dry out and itch and I had to buy another bathing suit because the chlorine in the pool had eaten through my favorite one. I began using dry skin lotion and I extended my swimming regimen for several more months.

In addition, several years ago I made a deal with my body that for each soul reading I did, I would devote one hour of attention to my physical well being. Since I enjoy diversity, I included walking, dancing, yoga, Tai Chi, gardening, sledding, playing Frisbee, as well as receiving pedicures, massages and acupuncture treatments.

My habit of befriending my body extended to writing and re-writing this book. I set my alarm clock to ring every fifty-five minutes to remind me to get up and take a ten-minute body break, which usually included walking my cats around the pond, weeding the garden, or picking fresh vegetables. Then I returned to writing.

I know that my body is my vessel for awakening and remaining awake. My ongoing story of strengthening and listening to my body includes a strenuous Pilates class three times a week where my teacher, Valerie Kitchen, reminds me that I have a flexible body and I need to gain stability and strength to add to my flexibility. Katherine Kates, my Qi Gong teacher reminds me to concentrate on softening my gaze and body in order to track my sensations and energy.

When you are centered in soul story your energy supports your breath, thoughts and actions. You have an inner sense that you are on the right track and often experience a sense of ease. People often feel a deep sense of contentment and inner peace. Simplicity reigns rather than confusion and drama that are often connected to personal story.

For example, last summer I checked on Craigslist for a house to rent for the summer. I spotted two places on a nearby lake. When I asked my body for a vote, I noticed that my shoulders stiffened, my breath felt labored and my heart was not happy with either location. I turned both possibilities down without another option. The next day a friend suggested I ask a mutual friend if he had a place available for my four cats and me. When she mentioned the possibility of living at the Gathering Place on 45 acres of forestland, I noticed that my shoulders relaxed, my breathing felt normal, and I laughed out loud—all green light signals from my body.

~Reflect on your responses to these questions:

- How do blocks show up in your body?

- What are the signals your body registers that tell you that you are reacting from unfinished business?
- What are the signals that your body registers that tell you that you are responding to a soul call?

Nervous energy is another ego signal. Focus on yourself long enough to track your energy. Train yourself to be aware of the flow of energy into and out of your body. It is relatively easy to identify which story you are starring in by noticing your energy, feelings, and attitudes. For example, when I notice myself rushing to make decision, I stop myself and remind myself that clarity often takes time. "Let me get back to you on this" has become my favorite response to a phone call bid for my attention. Another signal that nervous energy is running me is when I act impulsively.

Take time each day to notice yourself. This act of noticing is one of the most powerful steps to bringing about change. Here is a simple writing exercise to help you track your awareness.

- Date your entry.
- Now write the words, Right now I am aware of _____.
- Continue to repeat writing the phrase, "Right now I am aware of" until you no longer have anything to write.
- When you feel complete, read your list.
- Note what feelings arise.
- Write down any insights.

Researchers report that it takes twenty-eight days to change a habit. Make a commitment to follow through on this energy inventory for one month and discover how your story has changed.

We are often so busy or planning ahead for tomorrow that we are not aware of how other people affect our energy. If you slow down and make it your intention to gain awareness of the impact others have on your energy, you will become more conscious and grow in your ability to be a guardian of your own energy field.

It is relatively easy to spot an energy tangle when I am fresh from my morning meditation practice. My heart is open and my mind is clear and my body is relaxed. Harmony reigns. If one of my grandchildren slams a door and careens into my room, I am instantly aware of being impacted. However, if I am shopping and checking off items on my list and a friend spots me and begins to tell me the story of her most recent argument with her teenaged daughter, I might be too distracted to connect our chance encounter to a sudden drop in my energy.

On the other hand, have you met someone who radiates energy and invites you to get in touch with your light and you walk away from the brief encounter with a smile and maybe even a whistle? Or you might even feel inspired and you notice that people around you are responding to your positive energy.

Expand your energy inventory to include your relationships. Be aware of when and where and with whom you experience an abundance of energy. Similarly, be aware of when, where, with whom you experience a decrease of energy. When you discover that you are leaking energy, focus on the causes. Then ask:

- Why am I losing power?
- What is the pattern and the lesson?
- What is the deeper meaning of this energetic leak?

Then make a conscious choice to be around people who are empowering rather than people who are de-energizing. Here is a journal entry I wrote after completing an energy inventory:

Universe, I hereby resign from attracting and being with people who drag me down. I quit. It's over."

Remember that not only are you impacted by the energy of others, you are also influencing other people. My landlord delivered a package to me today from the UPS driver. He winked and said, "The rumor is you are the sweetest woman in Stetson, Maine." I was surprised.

⊕ Things To Do

Write for five minutes without stopping about what is bubbling up in your heart.

Try this reflection strategy as practiced by Ignatius of Loyola:

Personal Story or Soul Story: Your Choice

Identify the gifts and struggles in your daily life. Then respond to: In light of what's going on, how is life inviting me to move forward?

✺ Stretching Questions

What limiting beliefs that keep you glued to your personal story are you ready to let go?

When was the most recent time your ego got triggered?

Are you okay with being okay? If not, why not?

When and with whom do you avoid high beam living and loving?

What and who push you to live beyond the boundaries of your personal story?

Considering your skills, knowledge and experiences, what authority are you willing to claim?

♡ Quotations to Take to Heart

"There are no victims from soul perspective."
Big Angel

"Attentiveness is vital to waiting." Sue Monk Kidd

"We have been trained to not feel powerful."
Emmett Miller

"Your choices define your life." Rosalie Deer Heart

"Consciousness beyond ego is authentic Self."
Andrew Harvey

"Your goal on your path is to free everyone from your ego."
Andrew Cohen

"A role is nothing more than a coat." Lou Ann Daly

Chapter Two

Multi-Dimensional Nature of Consciousness and Beliefs

"We are what we think.
All that we are arises in our thoughts.
With our thoughts we create the world."

Buddha

The ABC's of Consciousness

WHERE we put our attention is where we put our power. If you want to know the present state of your consciousness, be aware of whom you are attracting into your life and what is happening for you. If you wish to shift from your personal story to your soul story, you need to re-program your unconscious mind. Both quantum theory and contemporary research in human perception suggest that over 80% of what we see in the external word is a function of our internal assumptions and beliefs. Therefore, what's happening in your external life mirrors your strongest internal beliefs.

Listen To Your Life

"I don't know who to call or go to. Nobody can help. I don't know if I have the strength to live," a friend's voice said on the other end of a telephone line.

Instinctively, I reminded myself to breathe into my high heart and connect with my guides and teachers.

"I do not always know when I am thinking negative thoughts. Sometimes I am not conscious of myself," she mumbles.

I breathed and reminded myself that ego is in charge of keeping us unconscious. Then I moved my energy to my high heart and asked my guides for a strategy to move Ella out of the victim role in her personal story. As usual my guides were available and clear. I passed their information on to Ella saying,

"Okay, here is your assignment. For the next twenty-four hours, practice repeating, God is _____ and fill in the blank. It is your responsibility to convince yourself of the truth of God's Presence. Nobody else can do that for you. That is your work and if you believe that your life is at stake, then it is."

Without a perceptual shift in consciousness and a new set of emotional options, we repeat the conditioned limited patterns regardless of new opportunities. You will know when you have transformed a limiting belief because both your perspective and your expression will expand.

For example, Barbara dreaded math classes in high school. She managed to avoid taking math courses in college and excelled in history and literature. When she was in her forties, she woke up one morning and knew she wanted to revisit algebra and geometry. Her parents thought she was kidding. Some of her friends decided she must be a walk-in. She signed up for an evening class and was delighted to discover that her art became more symmetrical and her paintings had more depth.

Richard was raped during his first year of college. He abandoned his dream of becoming a dancer and dropped out of college and joined the service. Bodybuilding became his obsession. He remained a loner and gained a reputation for being the toughest drill sergeant in the corps. He often said that "the gym" was his best friend. His secret remained his until he married and his first child was born. Then his dreams became filled with reminders of his assault. His wife became concerned because she felt that he was becoming distant. She invited him to do counseling with her. He agreed. Part of his recovery was to return to being a dancer.

All emotional turmoil is caused by the mind. If you are reacting, return to your thoughts. What is the false belief that created the reaction? All clinging and grasping is our emotional attachment to circumstances.

Wherever you are most wounded or ashamed, that is the place you need to re-visit in order to re-claim your body, voice, mind, vision, creativity and sense of aliveness. It's worth the effort. According to the ancient poet Rumi, "The wound is where the light enters you."

It's not always easy. Remember the ego will distort reality so it can have closure. Many people do not realize that their unconscious mind is stronger than their will power. Our unconscious is the home of our shadow self and it specializes in self-sabotage.

Our Shadow Self

Ego is a large part of our personal shadow that beats us up. Shadow includes those aspects of oneself that we do not want to see and therefore judge because they do not fit in with our self-image. Your personal shadow is not here to hurt you, but to point out where you are incomplete. Once we expose our personal shadow, it loses some of its control. Then we can move beyond it.

When we are not present, we risk projecting our unacceptable feelings onto others. Projection is an unconscious transfer of our own "unacceptable" qualities or behavior onto others so that they appear to embody those qualities that we reject in ourselves. Everything that we hate, resist, or disown about ourselves grows into our personal shadow. The shadow directs any act of personal sabotage. Projections get in the way of authentic communication and cause suffering. Carl Jung was right when he wrote, "Projections turn the world into one's own face." Identifying and taking back projections yields self-knowledge and empowers us to move beyond personal story.

I dread details—especially details and facts that are related to technology. My intuitive mind rebels and I judge myself harshly for having no tolerance. In the past my scared self ruled and I paid someone to do the technical work that my business required and my techno-phobic shadow grew bigger.

However, a few years ago I decided to learn how to build, design and manage my website. Three days a week I took my seat at the project table at the Apple Store and methodically created my website. I surprised myself when I surpassed my own expectations and added photos, videos, and several tabs. The day I helped someone else who was designing her website for the first time has a prominent place in my personal victory files.

Here are a few examples of shadow discovery and recovery. Marsha prided herself on her ability to connect with others. She was a natural networker. Yet she complained that her marriage was not working. She described her partner as "not present, distant, and self absorbed." She missed him and said she felt abandoned.

When I asked her if it were possible that she might be abandoning herself, she recognized her shadow. She made a decision to share more of her feelings and her excitement with her partner and she took the initiative to snuggle up with him in the evening. She even surprised him with a couples massage. No surprise that when she returned, she reported that he was much more present and available and they had decided to go on a second honeymoon.

Trudy was upset when she found out that her best friend was gossiping about her. She defended herself and said she had never said an unkind work about her friend and always maintained confidentiality about everything her friend said to her. When I reminded her that "always" and "never" are ego's words, she became quiet.

"Well, maybe, I slipped once or twice and repeated something she told me to another friend, but it was tiny compared to what she spilled."

"How is that not gossiping?" I asked.

"Guilty as charged," she replied.

"I don't want you to feel guilty. I want you to take responsibility for your own shadow material so you do not project it onto someone else and derail a friendship."

Brian was unhappy about his girlfriend who he described as "flirtatious—especially at parties. She laughs at men's jokes that aren't even funny, dances with anyone who asks her, and makes me feel like I am an idiot for being with her," he said.

When I asked Brain what his capacity was for flirting, he covered his mouth with his hands and muttered,

"Oh my God, I used to flirt outrageously before I met Matrice. In fact, that was what attracted her to me. It was fun and harmless."

"'So?'"

"Guess I have some thinking to do here. I would really be turned on if she flirted with me more."

I explained that once we acknowledged our own repressed shadow, we are able to see ourselves and others more clearly and connect more deeply.

Here's a way to bring to light your unconscious personal shadow.

- Make a list of people you do not like.
- Assign one word to each of these people.

- Acknowledge that you have created a story of your shadow, your own rejected qualities, which you project on the outside world.
- Out loud say, "I reclaim" to each characteristic you have listed.

Dr. Wayne W. Dyer, in *The Power of Intention,* writes, "Everything that happened to you is a lesson you can be grateful for. Everyone who came into your life was a teacher, regardless of how much you choose to hate and blame him or her."

There truly are no accidents. Even shadow wisdom teachers enter your life to remind you of what you value the most deeply. If you are committed to your spiritual journey, sooner or later you will encounter someone who will challenge every cherished belief, both spiritual and mundane, as well as your integrity, self-esteem and your patience. This person is your chosen shadow wisdom teacher. This person might teach you the reverse of what your soul values.

For example, I value friendships and community and my shadow wisdom teacher valued our relationship above all else. In other words, eventually you return to your inner soul values through embracing your shadow self. Or you may realize trust is one of your values by experiencing suspicion and distrust. If clarity is one of your soul values, you may experience confusion. If you value honesty, your shadow wisdom teacher might invite you to collude in ventures that lack integrity.

In my experience, shadow wisdom teachers are masters of impression management. Since intuition is one of their many resources, they excel at reading your energy. Remember that energy is information. Once they attune to your vulnerabilities, they work skillfully to become your ideal friend, lover, advisor, or colleague. For example, I value sensitivity, and my designated shadow wisdom teacher oozed empathy. I enjoy adventure, and my designated shadow wisdom teacher enthralled me with tales of intrigue and invited me to co-create a life of excitement. I appreciate knowledge, and he impressed me with his cognitive mastery. I value commitment and he overwhelmed me with devotion.

Other shadow wisdom teachers might also promise protection, advancement, or special powers, all the while feeding on your energy and light by demanding exclusive attention. Wherever you are vulnerable or have unfinished emotional work, you risk attack. Shadow wisdom teachers disguise their real motives while they manipulate and thrive on dominance and control. Publicly they may profess their generosity, love and even awe of you. Always look beyond the words to the behavior.

Here are some questions to ponder if you suspect you are under the spell of a shadow wisdom teacher:

- Are you growing in the relationship?
- How does your designated teacher treat you when you are alone?
- How does your designated teacher treat others?
- Does your designated teacher encourage your friendships with others?
- Does your designated teacher support you in pursuing your individual passions?
- Does your designated teacher honor your knowledge, values and your light?

Firing your shadow wisdom teacher can be a fierce struggle between your personal story and your soul story. Some describe the encounter as a life or death duel. Remember your designated teacher is an energy vampire and it is unlikely that he/she will cooperate with your desire to end the free banquet. Yet your commitment to end the toxic relationship is a desire to be free in your own energy and to realign with your soul purpose.

Remember that honesty and discernment are essential for self-mastery. Also, remind yourself that shadow wisdom teachers are skillful magicians. The first step is taking back your power and accepting full responsibility for attracting this energy vampire into your life. Next, take an honest inventory of your core vulnerabilities and any unfinished business in your life. Were you bored, lonely, scared, and ready for an adventure, without direction or seduced by an offer of financial abundance? Did you enjoy the attention or the pursuit? Be aware you might have been motivated by multiple needs.

Then surround yourself with compassion and send it to the wounded part of yourself that attracted your shadow wisdom teacher. As you let go of resentment, guilt, or shame you create more room for the energy of forgiveness. Take a moment and think about how you may have played the role of a shadow wisdom teacher for others in this lifetime. Next extend forgiveness to yourself and your teacher. Why? Resentment and judgment dim your light and decrease your ability to love yourself and others.

Now it is time to create a release ritual. Why? A ritual creates a boundary between who you were and whom you are growing into. It is an act of empowerment.

I wrote this journal entry about firing my shadow wisdom teacher for all time.

I walked to the deserted beach. The sun was high in the sky. It was almost high tide and the waves crashed to shore. I selected a large black stone and poured all the energy draining incidents that I associated with my shadow wisdom teacher into the stone. One incident that dimmed my light tumbled over another and another. When I felt finished with my story, I said out loud: I, Rosalie Deer Heart, from the Essence of my Being hereby dissolve and disintegrate all my links and cords with you from the past, present, and future. I breathed deeply into my belly and imagined letting go of my shadow wisdom teacher. When I felt like I had more room in my energy field, I continued:

I, Rosalie Deer Heart, from the Essence of my Being, now bless and release you to the schools of wisdom where you may grow within the light. I thank you for teaching me the consequences of not listening to myself, not loving myself, and for teaching me in reverse how much I value kindness, peace, love, creativity, and community. I command you to leave. Now. Then a very unlady-like noise arose from my belly. I repeated the breathing exercise a few more times to be certain I was free. Then I ran into the cold ocean and I flung the stone as far into the water as I could.

When I returned to dry sand, I breathed in and reclaimed qualities that are in alignment with my soul purpose. I giggled and moved my arms, legs, and hips as I breathed in the energies of clarity, self-love, trust, compassion, creativity, power, humor and joy. Then I celebrated my freedom by dancing barefoot on the wet sand. My return to myself felt like a glorious homecoming and I yelled, "Yes" to the universe and to my heart.

Looking back, if I had remembered to ask my intuition if the person who pursued me was in alignment with light, I may have saved myself much pain, isolation and soul searching. Then again, maybe the crash course offered by my designated shadow wisdom teacher was important. For sure, I recovered myself and learned to trust my instincts.

Light Shadow Teachers

We each have unconscious personal light shadows that are made up of qualities that we admire in others and have not claimed for ourselves. This too is projection. I married an artist. He was my light shadow. After we married, he never picked up a paintbrush again. He had a hidden inner belief (shadow) that he could not be both a husband and an artist. In retrospect, he played his part perfectly. Eventually I grew up and embraced my own artistic capacities.

- Make a list of people you admire.
- Assign a descriptive word to each name on your list.
- Acknowledge that you have created a projection of your light shadow.
- Out loud say, "I reclaim" for each quality on your list.

The Power of Negativity

Deepak Chopra, author of *Quantum Healing*, conducted a study at the National Science Foundation that revealed that deep thinkers think about 50,000 thoughts a day. The same study cited that the majority of what people think is 95% negative. Negative thinking, which is connected to our ego and our personal story, is an addiction that depletes our energy and impacts our consciousness.

Take a moment to appreciate the wisdom contained within this short interchange.

"I thought I would never get here, my friend said.

"I know and that's what took you so long."

The Multi-Dimensional Nature of Consciousness

Since consciousness is layered, being aware of the potential layers is essential, especially since past lifetime patterns, vows and karma hide out in our unconscious mind and our akashic records—the history of our souls.

Self-reflection is a lifetime skill. A past lifetime vow feels different in our bodies than resistance or a phobia. A past lifetime bleed through often feels as if we are in a trance or under a spell and the urge to repeat whatever the limiting pattern associated with the former lifetime is huge. Stay aware of yourself long enough to track your recurring patterns.

Past Lifetime Bleed Through

Past lifetimes and past lifetime vows exist within the realm of quantum thinking where all possibilities co-exist. Time is indeed elastic. Past lives are recorded as emotions that act as magnetic glue that gloms on to similar energy, feelings, or experiences. Imagine your present lifetime as a blank sheet of paper. Now place a clear piece of paper over your present lifetime. Let's name the paper on top your most recent past lifetime. Now place another transparency over the first one and let's label that your second most recent life time. We could go on and on adding lifetime upon lifetime until we had a large stack of pancake lifetimes.

Each of our past lifetimes is made up of energy and the energy of emotion is what triggers past lifetime themes to bleed through into the present lifetime. Some people refer to their unconscious behavior as "being on automatic" or "being taken over" as they responded to the past lifetime stimulus exactly as they had responded in the past.

When I do a soul reading, I remind people that energy is information and that energy follows need. Whenever a past lifetime overlay is present, the guides give me the lynchpin lifetime where the self-sabotaging patterns or blocks originated. The person's guides also provide information about how to integrate, release or heal the past lifetime so the person can be free in their energy.

The following examples of past lifetime overlapping illustrate how unresolved past lifetimes can infiltrate your present lifetime and chain you to your personal story.

In a recent session, Mark's guides challenged him to be in his power and visible so others might recognize his healing abilities and seek him out.

The dread I felt from the man facing me was palpable. He gulped, put his hands in front of his mouth and whispered, "You mean I cannot be a hermit any longer?" We both laughed at the irony of his question and then we settled into silence.

In my experience, once you recognize the truth and the power of an unconscious, underlying pattern, ironing it out is fairly simple.

"I do not wish to come back and be required to take center stage again," he said loudly. The emotion in his voice alerted both of us that he was reacting to something bigger than incidents from this lifetime. His guides flashed a past lifetime where he used astrology to forecast the future. Many sought him out for future predictions, especially auspicious battle dates.

His twin brother was jealous and determined to undermine him.

He consulted Mark who gave him accurate information about the time and place to win an enormous military victory. However, he deliberately lost the battle. Many people were killed. He saved his own life and used his defeat to discredit his brother. No surprise to either of us that his twin brother from the past lifetime has played the role of his nemesis in this lifetime.

Mark tortured himself about how he could not have foreseen his brother's defeat and then he accepted total responsibility for misguiding him. He felt disgraced and went into voluntary exile. He died without realizing that his brother had betrayed him. However, just before he died, he made a vow never to be in a position of knowing again.

When I described the dynamics of the past lifetime, he recognized his persistent self-sabotaging pattern this lifetime. He described how he tortured himself by maintaining silence especially when his intuition leaked through to his consciousness. He shut down and isolated himself to protect people he loved. Forgiving himself was the first step. Letting go of doing penance freed him to step into the fullness of his soul agreements this lifetime. Forgiving his brother was easier than forgiving himself. Letting go of all the dynamics of his past lifetime personal story brought a sense of peace and hope.

Shelly consulted me because she could not make up her mind whether she wanted to preserve her twenty-five year marriage or file for a divorce. Although she adored her three pre-teenaged children, she ached to live an authentic life. "When will it finally be my time?" she lamented.

She looked uncomfortable when she told me she had enjoyed an affair that awoke her sexual passion and she was no longer satisfied with her unfulfilling relationship with her husband. Earlier she had made the decision to leave her marriage to be with her lover, who she considered her soul mate, but he told her he was not interested in a committed relationship.

Since the affair, she questioned whether she would ever feel sexually excited or fulfilled in her marriage. Yet she refused to say out loud that her marriage was over. She questioned whether she had the courage to leave her husband without another man who cherished her waiting in the wings.

Although they started counseling, she protected her husband from the depth of her feelings because she didn't want to hurt him.

"Where did you inherit the false belief that pretending "to make happy or make due" was less painful to your partner than telling the truth?" I asked her.

Instantly, we both knew the original dilemma that was the cause of her rage and then inertia was deeply anchored in the past.

Returning to a previous lifetime was easy. Her guides showed me a recent lifetime in China. Her marriage was arranged when she was sixteen years old. Her heart belonged to another man. She remained a dutiful wife in a loveless marriage for forty years and kept her secret love private. When we explored the connection between her and her secret lover, she learned he was not the man she imagined him to be. She had hung on to an illusion for four decades. On her deathbed she made a vow to experience and explore her sexuality in the next lifetime— no matter what the cost.

In terms of the past life overlay, the point was not whether to remain married or get a divorce. The opportunity to resolve karma was to risk being honest and clear about her sexual desires. Authentic communication was connected to her soul purpose.

Carl's soul purpose was to balance practical living with mystical knowledge. He worked in a hospital and he was legendary for being practical and responsible. Then he completed a course in cranial sacral training and yearned to use some of the energetic techniques with his brain-injured patients. However, he resisted treating his patients with cranial sacral techniques because he feared his colleagues would think he was "bonkers."

His body trembled when he spoke of "exposing" himself to his conservative colleagues. His anxiety tipped me off that a bleed through lifetime might be the place to start. His guides opened a past lifetime when he had been a healer in hiding because some people had threated to expose him as being a devil worshipper.

As his reputation as a healer grew, he became more visible. His fear of punishment came true when he was killed for "practicing the devil's magic."

He had hard wired healing with torture and death. Integrating and teaching what he knows about the invisible ways of energy in practical ways both excites and scares him. Identifying and clearing the past life trauma allowed him to enjoy a fresh perspective without the overlay and expectation of repeated trauma.

Clearing Karma

Karma, like limited beliefs or past lifetimes, can restrict your light potential. The more you identify with your ego mind, the greater the tendency to repeat and reinforce the karmic patterns that restrict your freedom and cause you to suffer. Be aware that just as we inherited intergenerational family beliefs, we can also inherit ancestral karma. I equate karma with soul memory.

Carl came from a hard working family whose great grandfather emigrated from Russia when he was sixteen years old. He leaned how to speak English and began a small business. He took on a partner to grow the business and he went bankrupt. Skip forward one and two generations and Carl's heirs, his son and two grandsons, also established successful businesses that eventually went through bankruptcy. The power of ancestral karma can be huge.

I believe karma exists to integrate the teachings we need in order to open our hearts. Think of karma as a teacher who points out where your life is out of balance. Think about it as a lack of knowledge or clarity that resulted in unfinished business in a previous lifetime.

Karma results from non-choices or the negative choices we have made in the past. Karma is meant to be resolved, not accumulated. Releasing karma affects the future personality as well as the past one. Negative choices generate consequences to give us an opportunity to re-choose our actions. Once we make a positive choice, the situation does not recur because our spirit is no longer attached to the negative choice that gave rise to the lesson.

It is often difficult to identify your own karmic issues because karma interacts and restricts mind and perception. For example, karma creates limited thinking, which restricts our freedom to make choices. In case your ego successfully ducks, denies, or rationalizes your karma, other people will trigger the karma that you have not yet worked out. Karma can compromise your ability to be happy and enjoy life.

Here are a few examples of karma at work.

Shelly came from a family of women where pleasure and happiness were forbidden. Her grandmother married at sixteen and birthed three children in five years. Her mother was depressed and took her "little blue happy pills." When Shelly left home and went to college, she enjoyed herself for the first time.

She delighted in her sexuality and decided to do a year abroad in Italy because she found Italian people joyful and loving. Both her mother and grandmother warned her that happiness did not last and she would have to "pay the piper like everyone else."

Shelly fell in love for the first time and looked forward to getting married, raising a family, and living in Italy. Her mother gave her an ultimatum. She had to choose between her family and her future. Shelly had an abortion, returned home and continued her education. She no longer laughed and announced that she had her one shot at happiness and it did not last.

Jennie questioned whether she should leave her marriage of twenty years because a psychic had told her that her karma with her husband was complete.

She continued, "Besides he has such big energy. I feel like he sucks my life force right out of me." Then she cried.

When I reminded her that one of her life lessons was to define her power within an intimate relationship, she stopped crying. Then I said, "Do you imagine that if you were in your power that he could "suck your life force?"

"But you don't understand," she whined, "He is so good to me—the most generous man I've ever been with. He gives me everything."

"Then why are you miserable and complaining about him to me?" I asked.

She shrugged. One more time I asked, "If you were in your power how would your relationship look?"

She smiled and said, "I would not be with him."

We both sighed "Hmmmm" at the same time.

Robert described himself as empty and desolate. Then he sobbed and muttered, "Everything that I have worked toward for thirty years has been taken from me." Not surprising, his energy was very low. I asked him for permission to check his akashic records, which I think of as soul memory, for clues to his self destructive tendencies. I was shown a past lifetime when he had cursed his soul. Obviously that harsh judgment has ramifications that can resonate throughout lifetimes.

These suggestions help minimize karma from this lifetime:

- Be responsible for your thoughts, words, actions and behavior.
- Be honest and clear with yourself and others.
- Release grudges.
- Avoid power struggles.
- Move on when the energy feels like it is dying.
- Appreciate and celebrate the differences between women and men.
- Banish game playing and one-upmanship.
- Specialize in forgiveness of self and others.
- Become a magnet for compassion and joy.
- Express gratitude daily.

If we desire to be of service to others, we must begin with ourselves. Confronting all that is unfinished in our lives is the agenda. We must be willing to be an agent in our own transformation and do the clean up work before we offer ourselves to be of service with others. Wounded people attract wounded people and karma activates karma.

When I lived at Findhorn, an international community in rural Scotland, the two best selling flower remedies were Karma Clear and Manifestation.

The benefits of releasing karma include:

- Quieter mind
- Easier access to Authentic Self
- Increased emotional, mental and spiritual freedom
- More trust in self, others and the universe
- Greater capacity to give and receive love
- Heightened creative expression
- Magnification of awe and appreciation
- Increase in compassion and readiness to forgive self and others

My soul buddy Joan recently began a new relationship. She and her new partner, Chuck are both in their seventies. I congratulated them on their courage and faith. After a few months of being together, she called me and asked, "I don't think I have known Chuck in the past. Do you think that is okay?"

"Sure," I replied without thinking, "just be careful that you do not create karma together so you have to return again and work it through." We laughed.

Past Lifetime Vows

The truth about vows is that we make them and they serve us for that time and we can also break them when they no longer serve our present day soul purpose. However, few of us are conscious about vows we have made in the past. As long as we remain unconscious of their existence, they continue to feel like a spell and we are not free in our own energy.

Many past vows originated from lifetimes when we lived in religious orders or in communities dominated by strict religious beliefs. Although we no longer wear the garb of a spiritual community, we still may act as if we are under private vows.

I have become acquainted with thousands of vows during my three decades of doing soul readings. The following list contains the most popular ones:

- Obedience
- Stability
- Poverty
- Self Sacrifice
- Mediocrity
- Chastity
- Humility
- Invisibility
- Penance
- I will love you and only you forever and ever.
- I will never give up the fight.
- I will get even.
- I will never risk again.

Breaking vows takes courage. It is not work for sissies. In many cases the vow may feel as familiar as your breath. Releasing the vow means you are now no longer hobbled or role cast, and that means you have the freedom to show up for your soul purpose.

Vow of Stability

Donna's soul purpose this lifetime was to experience freedom and that included freedom to move forward, freedom to make her own meanings, freedom to play, freedom to discover who she is and freedom to validate herself. Yet her personal story lacked both a sense of freedom and energy.

"Each time I take a step forward towards my own freedom, my husband accuses me of being selfish," she complained.

"How perfect," I said to her. "You chose someone who mirrors and expresses your inner conflict."

She continued, "I stay in relationships way past the time I should. I have a habit of making do and inside I feel like I am dying. It is the same pattern in my career, with friends, in partnerships, and even the places I live."

I checked and she had a vow of stability from a past lifetime that she had not broken in her dying time. The vow of stability was originally a religious vow that said, I promise to never leave the order. The threat of disgrace and penance kept the covenant secure. The way a vow of stability can play out this lifetime is to work for the same company all your life, to remain rooted in a neighborhood or state that you have always lived in, or to remain in a relationship that is not fulfilling because you made a promise.

When I told her about her vow of stability, she said, "That makes total sense, Rosie. You would not believe how anxious I get when I even dare to think about making a change that I sense might allow me to move forward."

"I bet you panic," I said compassionately.

"Exactly," she said with tears in her eyes.

"This is huge," Rosie," she whispered.

"Yes, this is your jumping off place," I said and reached for her hand.

I carefully explained the vow breaking sequence because I was sensitive that we were entering a similar energetic pattern that was set up when she made her initial religious vows. I also explained that part of the ritual was blessing the vow because it had served her once upon a time.

Then I asked her to repeat after me, I, (and her full name) from the Essence of my Being, now bless and release the vow I made to stability. It is over."

Then I reminded her to breathe from the bottom of her belly in order to let go of the vow that had held her captive to an ancient personal story. I tracked her energy and was prepared to clap in her energy field to assist her to release the pent up energy if she needed more help.

After she had successfully released the past vow, we followed up with a reclaiming statement. By reclaiming aspects of ourselves that are in alignment with our soul's purpose and soul agreements, we re-magnetize and empower ourselves to be present for our soul's work.

When I asked her if she were ready to do the reclaiming, she smiled and said, "Absolutely." I laughed because she was showing up even before the ritual! I invited her to repeat after me, "I (and her full name) from the Essence of my Being, now reclaim my freedom, passion, beauty, and anything else that is in alignment with my essence. When she felt complete, I invited her to view herself in my big mirror. Let's see who is here?" I said.

Vow of Self Sacrifice

"My wife is threatened when I do something for myself. She went berserk when I started an exercise class. She is afraid I am pulling away and has convinced herself that we are headed for a divorce."

"And then what happens?" I ask.

"I usually cave in so she won't get grumpy. But that doesn't work either because I get angry at her and myself."

"How do you imagine this pattern of abandoning yourself is connected to the past lifetime vow you made to self-sacrifice?" I asked.

"But if I take care of myself and go off to the gym, she gets insecure."

"Do you have a spiritual responsibility to heal her insecurity?" I confronted.

"Sometimes I act like I do," he replied.

"That does not answer my question," I reminded him.

"I consider everyone else's needs more important than mine. Sometimes I feel like a wimp and I get scared that I will get depressed like my father."

I reminded him that acting on his own behalf was part of his soul purpose.

That means he would bump up against people who treated him like he had treated himself in the past.

A Vow of Mediocrity

Originally, the vow of mediocrity or anonymity was a religious vow to never stand out. This can show up again as a tendency to be invisible and avoid growing into your authentic self this lifetime. It can also masquerade as false humility this lifetime.

Gretchen had a vow of mediocrity that sentenced her to never stand out or to use her power. The vow showed up full-blown when she was in her mid-forties and unhappy in her marriage. She decided to have an affair rather than end her marriage. Eventually, her husband found out about the other man and he filed for divorce. The underlying power of the vow continued to sabotage her and she was fired from her job a few months later. She confessed that she hated her career and like her marriage, she did not take a stand by using her voice. Releasing her vow of never standing out and being present means she will be free to accept responsibility for her voice and her vision.

The True Love Vow

I will love you and only you forever and ever is another powerful vow that acts like a spell. If you have this vow in your energy field, you are not available to consciously love another this lifetime unless your beloved from a past life time shows up this lifetime, which is unlikely. Breaking this vow takes courage because you might be so caught up in this love vow that even the thought of releasing it makes you feel unfaithful and ungrateful, or hopeless that you will ever attract another beloved.

Making a vow is serious. It is not too late to make a vow that affirms your commitment to grow beyond your personal story and live into your soul story. For example, when I divorced, I knew I no longer wished to define myself by my ex-husband's name. I also knew I had grown beyond my maiden name. So I asked my guides for a name that would keep me connected to my spiritual path.

Not only did I change my name legally to Rosalie Deer Heart, but I also made a public vow that I would live the rest of my life with this name as my own—no additions, hyphens, or exceptions.

⊕ Things To Do

Since time is elastic, I invite you to design a future lifetime.
Then begin living as if you were already your future self.
Make a list of lessons learned and gifts received from events that you judged as failure.
Before you go to sleep, be aware of what you are looking forward to tomorrow.

☉ Stretching Questions

What is your capacity for confronting your projections?
In what ways have you served as a shadow wisdom teacher to others?
Do you remember any dreams that may be remembrances from past lifetimes? If so, what were the themes?
What vows have you made this lifetime? Did they add or detract from your wholeness?

♡ Quotations to Take To Heart

"The role of the impure ego is to make you believe that what is good is bad for you and what is bad for you is good."
           Muktananda

"How people treat you is their karma, how you react is yours."
           Wayne Dyer

"If the stock market exists, so must past lives."
           Margaret Atwood

"To speak with the shadow you must know the language of darkness."
           Mehmet Murat ilden

Chapter Three

Releasing Resistance and Claiming Freedom

"Spiritual growth requires you to become aware of everything you are feeling all of the time."

Gary Zulov

OUR personal story will accompany us until we die. Shift from personal story to soul story and your personal story becomes sacred. As we become more aware of our light dimming patterns and beliefs, we free ourselves to interact authentically and honor our soul agreements.

Toxic emotions bind us to our personal story. Hurt feelings serve as shock deflectors to dull our pain. If we hold on to them, they dim our light and distance us from our soul. Pain restricts love. Too much pain can cause suffering and eclipse enjoyment of life. Too much pleasure can lead to addiction.

To break through the lock down of personal story, we must be willing to confront our pain rather than to give into it and play out a victim role. The following story illustrates the power of a belief that almost immobilized a woman who wanted to break out of her personal story and move into her soul story.

Mimi: "I don't want to repeat getting a migraine headache the second day of the Embodied Soul Training and be incapacitated for the next two days of the workshop."

Me: "How about working together to identify the ego based belief that incapacitates you and causes you to stay in bed and withdraw?"

Mimi: "I believe that I can take in only so much love and then I have to shut down to protect myself. I know that it doesn't make sense to choose to be in pain in the midst of high loving energy, but that is what I do to myself."

Me: "Can you appreciate how that false belief connects you to physical pain and claims your energy?"

Mimi: crying, "Yes, and I don't want to be a hostage any more."

In order to transform a toxic belief, you must choose to adopt a higher frequency. Love and healing have a higher frequency than fear and shutting down. The key is to move beyond your ego, which keeps you small and scared, and align with soul.

Begin by cancelling the limiting belief. You can do this by speaking out loud in a commanding voice, "From the Essence of my Being, I cancel the limiting belief that I must shut myself down to protect myself as the energy accelerates."

Then align with soul by saying out loud, "From the Essence of my Being I affirm my ability and delight to remain fully present to give and receive unconditional love." Think of it as gardening. You pull the weeds (toxic beliefs and negative emotions) up by their roots. Then you plant new seeds (soul story), nurture them and enjoy watching them flourish.

Our feelings occur in our minds and in our bodies at the same instant. Every emotion has both mental and physical aspects that cannot be separated. Did you know that it is impossible to have an emotional reaction without first having a prior thought? Thought is living energy. Each thought affects our body, mind and soul by amplifying, depleting or being compatible with our life energy. There are basically only two emotions— pleasure and pain. Either it feels good or it hurts. Think of life as a river with two banks with pleasure on one side and pain on the other side. The easiest way to float down the river is to stay in the middle so you can move effortlessly between the two banks.

Light Dimming Emotions

Brene Brown and James Pennebaker, from the University of Texas at Austin, studied the connection between trauma, creative writing and physical wellness. They found that for people who held on to a secret trauma because of shame or guilt, keeping the secret had a worse effect on their physical well being than the actual traumatic event.

They also found that men generally respond to shame with anger and disengagement, while women have a tendency to turn shame against themselves.

Shame comes from an error belief that says: I am not good enough, lovable enough, smart enough, mature enough, strong enough, sensitive enough, or spiritual enough.

Frustration, anger, shame, arrogance, self-doubt, inadequacy and fear all have their roots in ego and can dim our light if we do not challenge the feeling and trace it back to its original source. Furthermore, convincing ourselves that we are inadequate can lead to dreaded feelings of shame and guilt.

Listen with your open heart to my personal story of an encounter with a medicine woman in Bali, Indonesia that illustrates the light eclipsing power of shame, guilt, and penance.

A balian specializes in healing and trance work. She also uses both black and white magic to cast or repel spells. Like the traditional pipe carriers in Native American tribes, her gate is always open to help anyone.

I waited for a week to meet her. In Bali, the calendar dictates specific days for trance channeling, healing, and spell casting rituals.

In trance, the petite balian shouted at me, "The gods say, do not marry again. Never. Do you hear? Never. Your healing gifts are many and they are not to be squandered on one man."
The force of her words surprised me, especially when I remembered her gentle manner during an earlier healing session. Yet her loud words resonated in my heart as Truth. She did not know I have two ex-husbands. She did not know I divorced each one when I felt separate from my soul. Wayan, the young male artist and translator, knew nothing of my hop scotch marital history.

Almost eighteen years later I sit before my open journal and I wonder what made me ignore the balian's initial warning. Was I rebelling? Was I under a spell? Was I resolving some old karma? I married again. Within eight months I felt exhausted. I also depressed myself by convincing myself that my healing abilities and intuitive resources belonged to my past.

However, upon reflection over many years, I understood that my healing energies and intuition never left. It was I who disappeared. I allowed myself to be swallowed up by my own shadow. I am still uncertain what returned first: my re-commitment to turn my life over to God, or my guides or my intuition. Perhaps it was a multiple simultaneous arrival! (As soon as I put the explanation point on the previous sentence, I sensed the presence of one of my guides.)

Guide: You have been doing penance for the past several years.
    Me: Yes, I have isolated myself, turned away from sculpting, abandoned music, refused to stay in contact with soul friends, and shut you out, too.
    Guide: *Not completely. We influenced you in dreamtime. Do you agree it is time to forgive yourself and begin to teach about self-love and soul purpose once again?*
    Me: Anger, self-blame and self-pity were intense. Forgiveness feels intense, too.
    Guide: *Intensity, in any of its many forms, has the potential to become an addiction. Let this clearing ritual be gentle and easy.*
    Me: I do forgive myself for not discerning Truth and for not taking action. I forgive myself for abandoning my creativity and my friends. I forgive myself for blocking my guides and turning away from my soul purpose. I breathe deeply and release my vow of penance. "Be gone," I bellow.

In order to assure myself that the release is complete, I say, "And I forgive myself for everything I did or said, even things I don't remember or have no words for."

Next, I inhale and then I let go of the deadening energy from my solar plexus. Then I sense a softening in my heart, but I know the release is not finished. I need completion. No room for error. I return to my intention to let go of the dense energies of penance and self-judgment. Again I breathe into my belly, hold my breath and forcefully exhale. Two more inhales and exhales and I feel free. However, I remind myself to take the next crucial step. To fill up the vacuum that I created in my energy field when I released all the aspects of penance, I breathed in and invited the energies of compassion, self-love and joy to fill my energy field with ease. And so it is.

Befriending Emotions

I was raised to be good, please others and be responsible. When I denied my feelings, especially the ones that did not feel good, I depressed myself. That's why I challenge you and myself with the question, "Would you rather be free or good?"

I have learned from my own experience that what we resist persists. The goal is wholeness, which is another word for freedom.

Begin by taking responsibility for whatever you are feeling. Befriending all feelings, no matter what they are, is the beginning of emotional freedom. In order to befriend your emotions, lead with curiosity not judgment. Getting to know a feeling allows you to track it to its source. Name the feeling. Breathe into the emotion. Consider responding to the following questions to help you track and befriend a feeling:

- What does fear, anger, self doubt, guilt, resentment and/or shame feel like?
- Where do you feel it in your body?
- What's it like to allow fear, anger, self-doubt, resentment guilt and/or shame to run through your body?
- How big a space does it occupy?
- What happens when you stay present with the feelings of fear, anger, guilt, resentment and/or shame in your belly?
- What is the source of this emotion in your life?

The most transformative way to approach the emotion is to keep your attention on where you need to go. For example, experiment with disengaging from the paralyzing energy of fear by taking action in the face of the fear. Fear does not allow you to breathe. What happens when you think about fear as excitement without breath?

There is an old saying: What do you do when you are walking in hell? Answer: Keep walking. Action realigns your brain patterns. Allowing yourself to feel the emotion means you are stretching to another part of the self that is not ego. Ask yourself if the story fear tells you rings true. Then ask yourself with a curious mind, "Is this a valid response right now?" It is not about getting rid of the butterflies in your tummy, it is about getting them to fly in formation.

Simmering

As a way of working with our aggressive tendencies, such as resentment that involves unresolved hurt, anger or both, Dzigar Kongtrul Rinpoche, in his book *The Power of the Open Question*, teaches the nonviolent practice of simmering as a way of gaining inner strength. We allow ourselves to wait, to sit patiently with the urge to act or speak in our usual ways and feel the full force of that urge without turning away or giving in. Neither repressing nor rejecting, we stay in the middle between the two extremes, in the middle between yes and no, right and wrong, true and false. Invite patience to sit with you while the emotional mud settles and your mind clears.

It's important to interrupt the spinning pattern. Stare back at the feeling or thought. Let it arise and then breathe. Next make it your intention to trace the thought back to its source. Then decide if the thought feels true for you now. Next ask, "Who would I be without that belief and the accompanying feelings?" Instead of asking, "What should I do or say?" stop. Take a conscious breath or two and ask, "Who do I want to become?" because your response will move you out of personal story and offer you freedom to align with your evolving soul story.

Listening and Letting Go

To disentangle from your personal story and your small self, practice re-directing your energy by choosing to stop complaining, comparing, gossiping, blaming and withholding forgiveness. Your capacity to let go of your prejudices, beliefs, control and feelings unconditionally determines how free you are. "Most people prefer the certainty of misery to the misery of uncertainty," says Virginia Satir, author of *PeopleMaking*. Please be aware that there is always a part of us that wants to avoid having a revelation because we will then be orphans to our own history.

- What emotion is your biggest obstacle to breaking free of your personal story?

- What important feelings are you not letting into your awareness? (Hint! Consider feelings that you might judge as not okay, for example, anger, jealousy and sadness.)
- Where in your life are you not telling the truth?
- Where in your life have you not kept your promises?
- In my relationship with _____, what do I need to say or do to feel complete and whole?

During my three weeks in Bali, Indonesia, one of our translators explained to me how the Balinese people honor all of their feelings.

When things are in front of us that cause pain
We reach out and put our arms around them
Then we bring them into our heart.

The Science of Positive Emotions

Connection, compassion and bliss are light expanding frequencies that connect us with our soul story. You might be surprised to learn that scientists are studying the vagus nerve because their research indicates it is the biological delivery system of positive emotions. The vagus nerve, which is at the top of your spinal column, merges through your brain stem deep within your skull and connects your brain to your heart. It is directly connected to prolific networks of oxytocin receptors involved in the experience of love and trust. Scientists can measure the strength of your vagus nerve by tracking your heart rate in connection with your breathing rate.

Dacher Keltner and Chris Ovens brought University of California Berkeley undergraduate students to their laboratory and measured vagus nerve activity while the students sat quietly. When they returned to the laboratory seven months later, they found that those students who scored high on vagal activity reported higher levels of social energy, friendships, kindness and a love for others. In addition, they reported more optimism and improved physical health. Their minds were more active in the aesthetic realm and when presented with images of harm and beauty, they reported greater compassion and awe. The most dramatic finding was an increased interest in transformative experiences that centered on the sacred.

If you are wondering, as I did, when I read this research, how you can increase vagal functioning, here's how:

- Massage
- Practice loving/kindness meditation
- Express compassion
- Extend gratitude

Positive emotions are contagious. Research proves that bystanders are affected positively when they witness an act of kindness. Here's a story about how I experienced this phenomenon one day while passing through airport security.

My story begins as I take my shoes off, load the gray buckets with my belongings and notice an elderly woman in a wheel chair in the line across from me as an attendant helps her remove her shoes and socks. Both of her bare feet were bandaged. I heard a security person announce over the loud speaker, "Random Check" just as I was about to push my bags on the conveyor belt for a security check.

When I realized that the frail, white haired woman in the wheel chair was the one to undergo a search, I watched more closely. An airport attendant leaned over her and told her he would help her stand up. She looked confused but obediently tried to stand up. I watched as she struggled to stand up. Her hands shook. I shuddered, noting that she was about five feet from the walk through security apparatus. Without thinking, I left my line and belongings and said to the security agent, "Please let me take her place. She is having a hard time even standing up." The security agent replied, "This is against airport protocol. Go back to your line."

I looked at the frail woman, who had returned to her wheel chair and said, "You announced this was a random check, right? So doesn't that mean you have no reason to suspect that the woman in the wheelchair is a terrorist. I am volunteering to let you search me instead."

"This is not your choice," he barked. "I will call my supervisor if you do not return to your line."

Motivated by kindness and aided by an adrenalin surge, or perhaps an active vagus nerve, I turned, walked behind the wheelchair and pushed

Releasing Resistance and Claiming Freedom

the silent woman to my original lane. The attendant waved her through. I returned to face the supervisor.

"What's going on here, ma'am?"

"Nothing now," I said, waving goodbye to the woman in the wheelchair as she left the security area. After I explained my actions, the uniformed supervisor said,

"He was only doing the job he is paid to do."

I smiled and replied, "I, too, was responding in the only way that made sense to me. That crippled woman might have fallen or panicked if he had forced her to submit to a random search."

"We train our personnel to do things by the book, Ma'am. He was following protocol."

"I observed that, Sir, and I asked your employee to make an exception based on age, fragility, and the fact that it was a random search."

"I could arrest you," he warned.

"Yes," I replied. "But in my heart I do not believe I did anything wrong. I guess that is my personal protocol."

He nodded, uncrossed his arms, and looked around at the people who were watching and listening. I had not noticed anyone but him and his employee. Then he motioned me through security. I smiled and said, "Thank You."

That could have been the end of the story, but it wasn't. When I arrived at my gate and sat down, a ticket agent approached me and asked to see my ticket. Still recovering from my recent stand off, I asked her why. She invited me up to the ticket counter. I feared my previous action meant I was being banned from flying.

Then she asked, "Where is your final destination, please?"

"Why?" I persisted.

"Do you have any layovers?" she continued, as if she too followed an invisible rulebook.

"Can I see your ticket, Ma'am?" she asked.

"As soon as you tell me what this is about," I said.

"Well, Ma'am apparently some man thinks you are a heroine. He overheard you when you told the security deputy your name and he followed you to this gate and pointed you out to me. Then he gave me a credit card and I upgraded you to first class."

"Where is he?" I asked, looking around the lounge area.

"He's not here. He had to make a quick connection. He wanted to re-pay your kindness. Happy New Year," she said and smiled for the first time.

I boarded the plane, took my seat in First Class, and ordered a complimentary glass of wine. Then I toasted the nameless woman in the wheelchair and the anonymous man who rewarded my kindness with kindness.

Kindness has a higher energetic frequency than fear, inertia or resistance.

I knew I could have gotten arrested and yet I chose to over ride my concerns about myself. If I had given into my personal story, I would have ignored the frail woman and rationalized my choice. Courage and a healthy sense of freedom accompany soul story.

Expectations and Self Esteem

How you feel about yourself determines what you think is possible.

Are you playing your life too small? Low expectations square with limited opportunities and sentence you to live within the limited narrative of your personal story. Four decades ago, Abraham Maslow introduced The Jonah Complex that exposed the many ways we evade our growth potential by setting low levels of aspiration and voluntarily crippling our potential as well as our destiny by engaging in pseudo-stupidity and mock humility. Maslow called this tendency to dim our light the fear of transcendence. Our personal ego is capable of holding our authentic self in prison as we cling to our limitations. One way to break up identification with the ego is to be aware of its motivations and then to dis-identify with it.

~Stop and listen to yourself several times a day for one week. The goal is to be aware of what stories you tell to others. Then consider what you notice by asking yourself these questions:

- Is my internal dialogue affirming or complaining?
- Does my inner conversation add to or detract from my light?
- If you are aware of a negative internal voice, ask, What historic toxic feelings and limited beliefs am I willing to release?

Then take a deep breath and commit to take one action that represents the most evolutionary response you can make.

Forgiveness Practices

Another way to halt personal story is to forgive whoever you are holding hostage and that includes forgiving yourself. That means surrendering your need to get even, be right or even understand. Think about the act of forgiveness as an exercise in compassion. Extending forgiveness frees others from your judgment.

Forgiveness allows us to free ourselves from the endless cycle of pain, anger and revenge that keeps us prisoners in our own suffering. But before you forgive, expect to grieve. Something precious has been lost and grief is a response to loss. You may experience sorrow, rage, fear or confusion. Forgiveness releases you from carrying the pain of the past. Withholding forgiveness creates blockages to the flow of energy. Forgiveness purifies the heart and frees the heart to love again.

~If you are ready to practice unconditional forgiveness, give yourself a hug and repeat the following sentences. It is okay to repeat a sentence more than once.

- I forgive completely all the people, known or unknown, who have hurt me throughout time.
- I ask anyone I have ever hurt, known or unknown, throughout time to forgive me.
- I forgive myself for any pain or suffering, known or unknown, I have caused to others.

While visiting the Edgar Cayce Center in Virginia Beach, Virginia, I learned about a short and effective forgiveness ritual that originated in Hawaii.

Take a conscious breath and imagine putting this ritual into action. Think of a recent time when you felt like you overreacted or misunderstood someone. You can phone them or in your mind imagine saying,

- "I'm sorry."
- "Please forgive me."
- "Thank you."
- "I love you.

Community Forgiveness Rituals

Mother Rita, who officiates at St John's Episcopal Church in Bangor, Maine, told a story about an annual forgiveness ritual that she participated in while she was on sabbatical in Russia. It happens in the Russian Orthodox Church the Sunday before Lent. She said the service was a combination of an Easter and Christmas service. People wait in long lines to take their turns asking forgiveness and extending forgiveness to all their neighbors.

Every one asks forgiveness and also replies, "God forgives you and me in turn." Mother Rita glowed as she described the ritual and then surprised us by enacting the ritual by asking the congregation for forgiveness for not always being all she could have been to the congregation. Her vulnerability was lovely to behold. I cried. We, in turn forgave her for not being perfect and we forgave ourselves, too. Driving home I wondered how my world might be different if I gathered a community and we did this forgiveness ritual. I believe we all could move more easily and deeply into our soul story.

Truth and Reconciliation Commission

You do not have to travel to Russia or Hawaii to participate in a forgiveness/healing ritual especially if you live in my birth state of Maine where on June 29th, 2012, five Wabanaki Chiefs and Governor Paul LePage signed a mandate document to initiate the Maine Wabanaki-State Child Welfare Truth and Reconciliation Commission. This historic document between Wabanaki Tribal Governments and the State of Maine represents the first truth and reconciliation effort within US territory that has been collaboratively developed between Indian nations and a state government to look at what happened to native children in foster care, many of whom were forcibly removed from their native homes by state agencies operating under the assumption that Wabanaki children needed to be civilized in white homes.

The impetus for the Truth and Reconciliation Commission comprises three key purposes:

- Truth—To document and create understanding between the Wabanaki and the State of Maine concerning what has and is happening to Wabanaki children in the child welfare system.
- Healing— To create opportunities to heal and learn from the truth

and to promote healing among the Wabanaki children and their families and the people who administered the program.
- Change— To act collaboratively on the information revealed during the TRC to implement system change in order to create and operate the best welfare system possible for Wabanaki children and their families.

On December 4th, 2013 in the Hall of Flags of the State Capital in Augusta, Maine, Robert Shetterly, a painter and creator of the decade long project of *Americans Who Tell the Truth* unveiled his two most recent works: portraits of Denise Altvater and Esther Attean, two Passamaquoddy women who are core leaders for the TRC movement.

In his talk an hour earlier, he spoke about the immense darkness of the native genocide, its unfathomable pain and grief, how it makes a mockery of the democratic ideals of this country, which is why people don't like admitting its ongoing legacy, which is why a formal commission of truth and reconciliation is necessary.

Arla Patch, a community organizer who was there told me, quoting Robert's words, what happened next.

"After several speeches, a former Department of Human Services case worker who had taken native children out of native homes and placed them in white homes, stood up and asked for forgiveness.

Silence.

Esther and Denise did not say anything to her at that moment --- how could you? Could you have absolved her as though you were priests? Of course not. When the event concluded, I went over to her and thanked her for her courage to speak up, to expose her own guilt and remorse.

She had just told me her name when Denise appeared and clasped her in a tight embrace. Then Denise drew back and kissed the woman's right cheek, then her forehead, then simply rested her forehead against hers and held that position of bodies embracing, foreheads touching —a complete connection of body & mind for a long time. Finally Denise took a half step back & continued to hold the woman's hands, just looking into her eyes. Both women were in tears. Nothing was said. But because of the intimacy of it, I said to Denise stupidly, "Oh, you must know each other? "

Denise said, "No, we've never met."

The woman began nervously talking about her career as a caseworker, how efficient she had been, how seriously she took the adoptions, how everyone came to her when they wanted something done."

Robert continued, "I could recognize the woman's courage and her pain, but had no legitimacy to offer more. What Denise had done was deeply consoling. Denise gave her something that words could not and that could only come from Denise, for Denise, now in her early 50s, had been forcibly removed from her home at the age of seven along with five of her sisters. What she offered could only come from the heart and soul of the victim. I have to assume that the woman felt forgiven. The agent is humbled by her remorse; the victim is empowered with her ability to forgive, to heal. Both are ennobled by the integrity of what they have given each other.

Here was what the TRC is all about. What happened was a moment of grace, a kind of matching of disparate but congruent pains that must be fit together if some healing is to take place. I then saw the TRC as a metaphoric altar, if you will— a sacred place which people can approach carrying whatever piece of this traumatic burden that they own, lay it down, and find reconciliation in seeing all those true pieces laid out together."

To learn more:
http://www.maine.wabanakitrc.org/about/documents/

Healing happens when we feel a loving energy flowing freely within us again. Frances Vaughan, author of *Awakening Intuition* reminds us, "As we ourselves are healed, we provide an example for others. And as we desire to help and heal others, we ourselves are healed. The result is that relationships become a temple of healing in which healing is recognized as a collaborative venture that leads to the recognition of our underlying unity."

As I was mid-way in the process of revising this chapter, I called the Edgar Cayce Health Spa in Virginia Beach to see if they had an appointment open for a massage later in the day. They did and I booked a session, intuiting that something profound awaited me.

The surprise took about ten minutes when Daniel, my masseuse, announced as he worked on my neck that he specialized in assisting people to release past lifetime trauma. Although I had done the emotional release work on having my neck severed in a past lifetime, the body memory remained in my neck. When I described the details of the brutal past lifetime, Daniel said, "I can help you let the trauma go and you can forgive those who killed you and claim your freedom to go on with your life." I sighed. He had no conscious knowledge that I was doing a final revision of a chapter on Releasing and Freeing.

"That's why I am here," I said with emotion.

As he massaged and supported my neck, he led me through a forgiveness and healing sequence, all the while reminding me that I was safe. When I acknowledged that my persecutors were mad with anger, I was able to see them more clearly. After I forgave them, they disappeared from my energy field. Breathing in the healing white light was the next step. I said out loud, in wonderment, "I am entitled to receive healing energy," and I allowed the healing to move into and through my body. The muscles in my neck spontaneously released and I felt like I had surrendered a long legacy of withholding healing from myself.

Outgrowing Personal Story

As your consciousness expands, so does your story. Dimming our light is our ego interfering with our spaciousness. We have incarnated to be more than space holders. Each of us has a unique role to play in furthering evolution. Each of us co-created our unique cosmic report cards with God. As we remember our soul agreements and our innate Goodness and live into our authentic selves, we align with our inner light and become mirrors of Divinity.

Here's what my guides had to say.

Open your heart and your energy field expands. If you stay in ordinary consciousness, you will receive precisely what you believe. If you open your heart you will receive more light and possibilities. Be welcoming, filled with positive expectancy and love. Be willing to bypass your little mind, which sometimes bullies as well as controls. By welcoming the as yet unknown future, you open yourself to revelations and the experience of co-creating the future, which you desire.

Be aware of any unfinished business that prevents you from moving away from your personal story. I conduct a completion inventory a couple of times a year. Like donating clothes that no longer fit or inspire me to Goodwill, I take an honest look at my life. My purpose is to let go of any deadwood.

~Note the predominant people, the predominant themes, and the choices that you made and did not make. Then answer the following questions:

- What did you manifest?
- What regrets do you have?
- Who or what got left behind?
- What are you grateful for?
- What illusions did you surrender?
- What was left unfinished?
- What brought you a sense of fulfillment?

At some point in our life, the story we are living becomes too small. Our personal trance ends and we can no longer pretend. Gradually we gain perspective and acknowledge that ego is an out-modeled strategy rather than hard evidence that we are bad, unloved, incompetent or hopeless. Know that when you grow tired or bored with yourself, you are on a transformational threshold. Our capacity to let go of all the outdated, contracted beliefs and personal dramas unconditionally determines how free we are. Remember that the voice of ego asks, "What should I do?" and the voice of soul asks, "What would I enjoy?'

Charles Eisenstein, author of *The Ascent of Humanity*, summarizes the shift in consciousness:

> "The story of powerlessness and separation simply won't be captivating anymore! In its place we will have a story of connectedness, of inter-being, of participation in the all-encompassing circle of the gift. And part of this story is actually a meta-story, a story about stories that invests all of our stories with creative power and motivates us to be conscious in their telling."

Think of movement from personal story to soul story as a movement from self-centered to spirit centered. When we awaken to our soul story, we are connected to Source-not as creatures but as co-creators.

Poet David Whyte points to living our larger story in this poem.

> "You must learn one thing.
> The world was made to be free in.
> Give up all the other worlds
> Except the one to which you belong.
> Sometimes it takes darkness and the sweet
> Confinement to your aloneness to learn
> Anything or anyone that does not bring you alive
> is too small for you."

Your Turn

Now it is your turn to challenge yourself to move beyond your limiting beliefs in order to experience more freedom to live into your soul story.

- Make a list of all the reasons you convince yourself that you cannot change, or move ahead into the future with clarity and confidence.
- Identify your strongest limiting belief that you act on to protect yourself from growing and knowing.
- With a sense of curiosity ask yourself, "How am I the source of my current life experience?"
- In what ways have you created the perfect scenario to move beyond your personal story?
- What is one choice you can make today that will move you ahead?

Here are a few guidelines that I have found helpful as I maneuver my way out of the morass of my personal story:

- Adopt a curious, playful mind.
- Speak, listen and act from a place of love.
- Focus on positive thoughts and release judgments and resentment.
- Welcome synchronicity and paradoxes and remember to inquire about the deeper meanings.
- Identify the areas of your life where you feel expansive and areas of your life where you feel contracted. Then take action.
- Take up residence in your high heart and connect with your guides and inner wisdom.

- Find at least one soul buddy who will challenge you to be all that you can be.
- Welcome all people and all events as spiritual teachers.
- Exercise and honor the needs of your body.
- Eat healthy, high vibrational food.
- Commit to a spiritual practice and be consistent.
- Journal about what is in your heart.
- Adopt gratitude, generosity and grace as your best friends.

I was uncertain how to wrap up the first part of this book. I have learned better than to try to contrive a conclusion to satisfy my ego. Hanging out with a bit of anxiety seemed like a grown up choice. So I acknowledged that I was clueless and I also wanted to be inspired. Poet Wallace Stevens often comes to mind when I am living in the in between space between not knowing and knowing. His advice, "Sometimes a walk around the lake is the best solution." It worked.

Thirty-six years ago I read the following excerpt from Morris West's *The Shoes of a Fisherman* as I threw the ashes of my son Mike into the ocean at Two Lights State Park in Cape Elizabeth, Maine. The words fell out of a book today as I returned from my walk around the pond and they feel as poignant today as the first day I read them:

"It costs so much to be a full human being that there are few who have the enlightenment or courage to pay the full price. One has to abandon altogether the search for security and reach out to the risk of living with both arms open. One has to be like a lover and yet demand no love in return.

One has to acknowledge pain as a condition of existence. One has to court doubt and darkness as the total cost of knowing. One needs a will stubborn enough in conflict, open always to total acceptance of every consequence of living and dying."

I believe that West has described how to live high beam within our soul story. Remember that soul story is living a life that reflects your true talents and gifts, your deep yearning, and claiming your highest potential. Your soul story is connected to expansive expression, creative service and healing. Fully flourishing is full engagement with life. One of soul's goals is to shine with purpose and passion. If you aspire to this path, carry sunglasses to give to others who need to shade their eyes instead of lowering your light.

Releasing Resistance and Claiming Freedom

In order to move into soul story, you have to make the choice to disengage from your small historical self. The in-between places between personal story and soul story are ripe for transformation. Think of them as places to grow potential. Since the universe always says, "Yes" to our strongest beliefs and predominant emotions, about ourselves, others and the world, now is the time to be clear about what you wish the universe to say yes to in your present life.

Bridging is one way to step out of a way of being that has become root bound and uncomfortable. The bridging process requires you to sacrifice your small story that has defined you, empowered you socially and also limited you. The transition from ego story to soul story is summarized in the following poem:

We do not arrive, we process.
We do not learn, we remember.
We do not become, we are.

⊕ Things To Do

- Practice every day doing three things that make you happy.
- Imagine a stranger asked you to introduce yourself by "telling your story." How would you respond?

    Tell the story from a victim's perspective.
    Tell the story from an empowered perspective.
    Tell the story from a comedian's perspective.
    Tell the story from God's perspective.

- The following exercise may help you to clarify some of your blocks to loving yourself: Write "I am afraid of…for five minutes without lifting your pen from the paper. Take slower, measured breaths in and out without pausing in between. This is called circular breathing in which inhale and exhale are connected. This breathing bypasses the inhibitions of the conscious mind. Next look over your list and ask "So what?" after each fear. Continue asking "So What?" until you transform your fear.

⚙ Stretching Questions

How Would Your Life Be Different IF

- You acted as if empowerment is the process of letting go of all limiting beliefs, wounds and regrets, that you allow to rob you of your light?
- You embraced the principle that nobody can give you what you are unwilling to give yourself and made a commitment to love yourself unconditionally?
- You substituted "I choose to" for "I have to?"
- You practiced being more curious than afraid?
- You dared to move beyond your inherited limiting beliefs to become a magnet for attracting the future you wish to embody?

♡ Quotations to Take to Heart

"Those who do not know how to weep with their whole heart don't know how to laugh either." Golda Meir

"Fear is what prevents the flowering of the mind."
                                                Krishnamurti

"The false self must be abandoned before the real self can be found."
                                                Sri Nisargadatta Maharaj

"Whenever possible ego will substitute erotic experience for unitive experience." Gerald May

"Life is meant to be a playful search for the truth."
                                                Edgar Cayce

Part Two

Bridging Personal Story and Soul Story

Chapter Four

Bridging Personal Story To Soul Story

BRIDGING into your soul story often brings surprises. If anyone had told me I would be able to levitate as I moved more deeply into my soul story, I would have told them that they had the wrong channel. The first time it happened, I was amused. I was home by myself. I was aware of feeling a bit light headed and although I have never had laughing gas, I imagined the feeling was similar. Other than the phrase, "lightness of being," I have no way to describe my physical sensations.

I gradually became aware that my body was no longer sitting in a chair, and I was approximately four inches in the air with no visible means of support. When I realized that my bottom was resting in mid air, I worried about how I was going to get back to normal since I had no clue how I had managed to lift off the chair. Within minutes I had descended and tried to figure out whether I was hallucinating or actually levitating. I tried to think of someone I could call to talk about this—preferably someone with experience. Nobody came to mind as a levitation mentor and I thought most of my friends would think I had gone off the deep end if I told them about my latest adventure with energy. In time, I learned to smile throughout the process. Leading with my curiosity, I played with steering myself while in midair when I knew nobody would be home. Without bragging, I taught myself how to navigate up the fourteen stairs that separated me from the first floor, but I never dared to try navigating the stairs going down.

During the six months apprenticeship, I never learned how to lift off consciously. It continued to happen at unpredictable times. My friend, Nancy Carlson, asked me to tell her what she should do if it happened during a public chanting session. I had not even considered that it could happen in front of others since it never had.

"I think you should just let me be. I always come down. But I don't think it is good idea to interfere with a natural process." She agreed and we both hoped that my levitation adventures would continue to happen in private.

The only time I had a small audience was the day I went to see a movie at the Bangor Mall Cinema. I arrived early and the theater was semi-dark. Only a few people were there and I decided to do a short meditation while waiting for the main feature. I was not aware that I had levitated until I felt a hand on my back and someone saying, "Excuse me. I just needed to make sure you are okay. You were growing taller and taller and then you shrunk. Is that normal for you?" the lady in back of me asked.

Without thinking, I replied, "It must be the light." (Then I giggled because of course it was the light, but not necessarily the dim theater light.) "I was just sitting here waiting for the movie to begin like you."

She looked from me to the man she was with and I knew she did not buy my explanation. That was the only time I levitated in public. Even now I have no idea of the purpose. The practice lasted for six months and stopped as suddenly as it began. I'm not sure why it happened—perhaps only to show me in practical terms that anything is possible.

The Benefits of Bridging

Bridging personal story with soul story moves you beyond the boundaries of your previous identity into a territory of expanded possibilities. When your ego directs the story, you are merely an actor assigned to one role. When your soul directs your story, you move out of the magnetic pull of your personal history into a place where you choose the roles that you wish to play. In order to bridge into your soul story, you have to release your outgrown personal story. Be aware as you move into your soul story you will no longer belong to yourself in ways you are used to because you have moved beyond the grasp of your personal history.

The challenge is to separate from old attachments and strengthen new ways of being even as you tolerate uncertainty. In the letting go process, be prepared to examine your personal beliefs about who you are supposed to be, how the world is supposed to work, and how others are supposed to relate to you.

In order to bridge personal story with soul story you must be willing to be aware of yourself long enough to translate insight into action and that takes focus, intention and will. When you acknowledge that you have a responsibility for creating the circumstances of your life, you are then in a position to move out of the victim position of personal story and bridge into the creator and vessel role of soul story.

For example, I lived through bankruptcy this lifetime. I felt ashamed and isolated myself. Shame sucked my light and kept me hostage to my personal story. I felt like I had suffered a siege of "spiritual amnesia" and had lost any memory or hope that a soul story co-existed. I knew it was important to feel all my feelings. I chose to live with all of my conflicting feelings without taking medication even though I knew the process would take more time. I was adamant that I would not do a spiritual bypass. In case you are unfamiliar with the term spiritual bypass, it refers to the act of choosing to focus on only love, light, and goodness and avoid dealing with whatever needs your attention.

Many months later I forgave myself and acknowledged my responsibility for co-creating the financial fiasco. I made promises to educate myself about money and avoid taking a financial risk beyond my capacity to succeed. I vowed that I would assert myself when I sensed something was wrong, no matter how my partner might react.

For him, "our" bankruptcy was the second entrepreneurial challenge that did not work out. He did not take the event personally. For me it was a life experience that I was determined never to live through again.

Unwrapping the event many times allowed me to take responsibility for myself and strengthen my business skills.

~Ask yourself this question: How was a specific event that you judged as toxic actually good for your growth?

Remember to be compassionate with yourself as you break through from your personal story to embrace your soul story.

Staying Present For the Whole Story

Recently, I met with a woman who had been sexually abused in her childhood. She told me how hard she had worked to forgive her abusers and move on with her life. Still she felt there was something missing. Healing seemed just out of reach.

When I listen to people's stories with an open heart, I empty myself of all my thoughts and am comfortable to wait in stillness. Then my compassion kicks in and eventually words come.

When I asked her gently if she was still holding on to somehow believing she could have prevented the assaults, all of her "if onlys" spilled out. I encouraged her to voice them all. When I sensed she was ready to reclaim herself, I asked,

"I wonder if you have forgiven yourself?"

She reached out and grabbed my hands and held on tight, "That's it," she said. "I have forgiven everyone else and forgotten myself. I was what was missing." Then I told her about a Native American belief that bears guard the spirits of anyone who has been abused and when the person is ready the bear returns the spirit.

She nodded and began to pray to the bear for the return of her spirit. I watched silently while Arnette completed her journey back to her wholeness.

The Love Bridge

Creating a new relationship with yourself that is loving, empowering and compassionate is another way to bridge stories. In order to align with our soul, we must make room for another way of relating to our life. Love has a stronger frequency than pain, fear, worry and jealousy, which indicate that you are starring in your ego story. To let love in requires us to melt. Unconditional love requires us to empty our minds and take off all our ego masks. One of my favorite chants is: Melt me. Mold me. Fill me. Use me.

I dare you to invite love to open you to your larger, sacred story. Love's primary goal is to support you to evolve beyond the boundaries of your previous identity in order to connect with your Authentic Self.

My guides have channeled about love for almost four decades and their love messages are sprinkled throughout my journals. This channeling popped up as I looked for love excerpts in my journal:

Love the hushes.
Love the loudness.
Love the people who love you.
Love those who do not express their love for you.

Love the adventure.
Love the solitude.
Love the unknown. Love the details.
Love the winter sky.
Love the cats that fill up the litter boxes.
Love the opportunities that arise.
Lead with love.
Learn through love.
Laugh at yourself with love.

My last book, *Awaken* was about awaking to love.

Here are a few of my favorite quotations about love that I found scattered throughout my journals:

"What has a soul to do but love?" Saint Theresa

"You cannot steal love or copy love. Love only lives in those hearts who can give themselves fully." Hermann Hesse

"Love is the way I walk in gratitude." Course in Miracles

"Only love can put you in a state of bliss." Miguel Ruiz

Love is our reason for being and through love every challenge can be transformed into a higher vibration. My soul's purpose is to love my life without exceptions. Opening your heart and living your soul story involves inviting and allowing others into your heart and meeting them more fully. Each time you choose love, you raise your vibration and that impacts the energy fields around you.

Here is a love inventory:

- Make a list of all the people you love.
- Review your list and note what kind of love you give and receive from the people on your list.
- Check in with your heart to discern if there are different expressions of love that you wish to welcome into your life.

The following poem by Madeleine L'Engle, author of *An Acceptable Time,* reminds me of the abiding presence of love

> To learn to live is to be stripped of all love
> until you are wholly without love.
> Because until you have gone
> naked and afraid
> into the cold dark place
> where all love is taken from you,
> you will not know
> that you are wholly within love."

Synchronicity and Quantum Living

When we choose to live our lives from a place of possibilities, we are often surprised by synchronicities. Our small scared self gradually transforms into our capable self. It is important to let go of figuring out how you are going to sustain your soul story. Content yourself with taking one step at a time trusting that when you have settled into the possibilities of your soul story, you will experience yourself making cosmic leaps. Saying Yes to a soul calling means letting go of what you thought you knew and opening yourself to thinking quantumly.

According to quantum theory in which all things co-exist simultaneously, all probabilities also co-exist for nature to be in harmony. Each choice (or future) lies in a state of rest until it is awakened by choices made in the present. All the possibilities that are not made continue to exist in parallel worlds. For example, if I set an intention to meditate every day, that intention co-exists with a variety of other possibilities like rejecting a meditation practice, remembering other life times when I meditated, and forgetting about my intention to meditate.

Quantum thinking, which is connected to our soul story, involves implementing new ways to maximize our mind consciousness. The more you grow in your ability to think quantumly, the more you will expect things to happen that have never happened before—even things you did not believe in. For example, nothing in my life experience prepared me for my third eye popping open, or merging with an angel, or channeling people who are dead, who I relate to as "Inspirited Ones. God gasps (Oh, my God!) and surprises erupt as we become more comfortable entertaining multiple possibilities.

One of the intriguing principles about quantum thinking and living is that there are no rules. The following list illustrates the differences between ordinary thinking and quantum thinking:

- Unlimited possibilities replace linear thinking
- Experience replaces knowledge
- Both/And replace either/or
- Intimacy replaces independence
- Connection replaces being right
- Co-creating replaces winning/losing
- Discovering replaces knowing

Emerging Soul Story

Alicia bragged that she has come into this life "kicking and screaming." She considered killing herself but never took action. Conscious partnership was not a valued part of her life experience although she was the mother of four children. Her predominant belief was that she had been drafted into this life.

In her late fifties she connected with an energy that she described as The Divine Mother and had a mystical experience. Awakening to her soul story was a surprise and she promised her new guide that she would remind others of the ever-present divine feminine. This unexpected event ended her identification with her struggle that was the theme of her personal story.

We don't always know what is in our highest good when we say a big Yes to life. There is a distinct difference between feeling good and experiencing the highest good. For example, I sometimes feel good after I have purchased a pair of new shoes. However that temporary good feeling does not match the way I feel after I have volunteered in the local elementary school. It can all come down to the after taste. Be aware of your sense of the after taste that follows a decision or action. When we begin to taste the person we are capable of becoming without limitations, we are also aware that we are capable of making a powerful impact on our life.

Easing Ego Out

While driving to a friend's house for supper, I drove past a middle-aged woman who stood on a concrete island in the middle of the busy intersection in downtown Portland, Maine. She had her hand out for money. I planned to stop and give her some, but the light changed and drivers behind me began honking. I drove past without making eye contact.

I could not get her out of my mind. Later I offered to pick up Italian sandwiches for supper. The shop was near where I had seen the woman earlier. It was almost dusk. I spotted her at the same intersection. This time I stopped and handed her ten dollars.

She looked at me and said, "Thank you. I can eat supper tonight."

I felt tears on my face.

She continued, "I like your shirt. I have one on that looks a lot like yours. Want to see?"

I nodded, embarrassed by my tears and not understanding what was happening.

I watched as she took off her down jacket, pulled a heavy sweater over her head, and took off another layer of warmth.

"I forgot that I put on so many layers. It gets cold out here on the street when the sun goes down. Finally, I got to it," she said. "See how it sparkles just like yours."

My heart opened. I felt her essence and her goodness.

I squeaked out the words, "We have good taste."

I had worked earlier in the day. Someone had paid me in cash. The envelope was beside me on the seat. I reached in, found the hundred-dollar bill, and handed it to her.

She opened her hands and said, "Thank you. I can eat for a week now. You are very kind."

I wanted to tell her so many things like she was kind and I don't know why I am the one to have a hundred dollar bill while she has little or how excited I felt to give away money. The honking of cars behind interrupted me again. She waved. I waved back. She may never know how deeply she touched my heart. Perhaps by telling her story, she will.

Crises As A Jumping Off Place

Often times a crisis is the catalyst that moves us out of personal story into soul story or vice versa. One can also move you from personal story to soul story or from soul story to personal story. Once again, all depends on what you see, how deeply you allow yourself to see, and what you do not see.

According to Alan Jones, author of Soul *Making*, the three crises include:

1. The crises of meaning: What should I do with my life?
2. The crises of betrayal
3. The crises of emptiness or absence

The way we respond to crises determines if personal story or soul story is in the foreground. For example, I met with a woman who recently discovered her husband of thirty years was having an affair. She insisted he leave their home. He did. Her friends expected her to be angry, devastated and inconsolable. Instead she felt exhilarated and free to create a whole different life. She explained to me that she would never have left the marriage because her wedding vow was sacred. His affair gave her permission to move into her soul story. When he returned home after three months, she was surprised. He told her that he had made a terrible mistake and asked her to forgive him and take him back. She knew if she agreed that she would slip back into personal story and she would not be happy with herself or him. She affirmed her readiness to move into her soul story and helped him move out.

Pain and illness often serve as bridges. Many years ago, when I lived in northern New Mexico, I was bitten by a brown recluse spider. Their venom can be lethal. The week before I was bitten, a man in the neighboring town had died from a bite.

A *curandera*, a native Hispanic healer, who also had been bitten long ago, as had her mother before her, soberly explained to me through an interpreter, that I now carried spider medicine. It had the potential to allow me to see into the center of creation if I chose to live. That was moments before I lost consciousness and traveled to another dimension. I thought I was dead when I became aware that I was in the middle of a life review.

The spider's venom gifted me with a vast witness perspective. I felt like my consciousness was wide-awake and I discerned the differences between personal story and soul story with one pointed precision. While out of my body, I remember feeling sad about several incidents where I chose to align with my personal story at the expense of soul story. First hand, I re-experienced from the witness perspective how I rationalized and reinforced patterns of withholding forgiveness to others and myself. Then I experienced how lack of forgiveness created blockages to the natural flow of my healing energy. I vowed—no more allegiance to my personal stories. My heart sprang to life as I extended forgiveness.

I am convinced that my soul gave me a second chance. I remember the exact moment when I understood with every cell in my body what T.S Eliot, author of *The Wasteland* meant when he said, "We are a soul. We have a body."

I do not remember when or how I realized that I was not dead. I did understand that I had the choice to return and transform some of the sticky places of my personal story or to die and heal myself in another dimension. Because I was raised to be responsible, I chose to return to my life and to transform my personal story. Before I returned to my physical body that was ravaged with fever, I heard myself agree to challenge myself with two questions when I was aware of the first nuances of ego seduction:

What is the most evolutionary action I can take at this moment?

What is the most compassionate response I can make?

My answers to those two questions expand my focus and invite a spiritual perspective. For sure, I appreciate the wisdom evidenced in this quotation by Norm Shealy, author of *Soul Medicine:*

"Healing, mediated by consciousness, and activated by intention, occurs when the patient's energy system is triggered to conform to the soul's blueprint."

Here are some suggestions for bridging into soul story that have worked for me. Use my suggestions as springboards for creating your own maps of irresistible ways to engage more deeply with your soul story.

- Engage in acts of self-love daily.
- Cultivate curiosity and befriend the unknown.
- Banish all beliefs that keep you small and limit your light and vibrancy.
- Experience yourself as ALREADY neck deep in grace.
- Give a 51% vote to your intuition when making decisions.
- Be aware of the joy potential each time you make a choice.
- Savor silence at least once a day.

Bridging Personal Story To Soul Story

- Make peace with imperfection—your own and others.
- Laugh out loud at least five times a day.
- Invite your dreams to remind you of all of who you are.
- Act intentionally by inquiring if your response is motivated by ego or soul.
- Collect ten hugs a day.
- Delight God.
- Play with your unique form of creative expression.
- Express gratitude upon awaking in the morning and before sleeping at night.

Dreams as Bridges

One night I had a dream and the only trace of the dream that I remembered upon returning to waking reality were the words "Unbounded Grace." No images. No emotional reactions. As I walked through my day, I murmured the words out loud, rolling them on my tongue, sometimes whispering them as if the sound of my voice might stir up more recollections.

When I resumed filing on the large peach alabaster stone that had occupied my attention for a few weeks, a faint form emerged. I was curious. It looked like the beginning of a wimple, a scarf that nuns wore over their heads in the 12th century. I resisted the thought of sculpting another nun. I put down my file and decided to take a brisk walk reminding myself that creativity is supposed to be about flow—not control.

When I returned, I examined the 16 inch variegated stone from all sides. No question a figure was emerging. What was I resisting?

The answer arrived the moment I posed the question. I surprised myself by saying out loud, "The last nun I sculpted took two years. I am finished with nuns. I want this piece to be playful and whimsical."

Resisting thrusts me in the center of personal story and causes suffering while surrendering is the bridge to soul story. When I admitted that I have experienced sporadic grace this life time and I was a bit daunted by the thought of unbounded grace, I was surprised to discover an inner willingness to move out of the lockdown of personal will into a willingness to experience a more expansive perspective. Then I surrendered and allowed the stone to become what it was meant to be. I chuckled as I patted myself on my heart and said out loud, "After all, I am a vessel." Letting go of how long the process took or even what form it might take made me giggle.

⊕ Things To Do

Listening For The Heart Beat in Your Writing

- Take a few gentle breaths and relax into your high heart.

  - Write on your paper or your computer, "Thank you for giving me information about what is yearning to evolve within me."
  - Record what you are feeling, hearing, and knowing.
  - If you run out of words, breathe into your high heart and write thank you, thank you, and thank you until the words begin to arrive.
  - When you are finished writing, read your guidance out loud.
  - If you are willing, make a commitment to put the words of wisdom into action immediately.

- Chose a situation in your present life that is a challenge.

  - Write about it from the perspective of why is this happening TO you?
  - Read your narrative out loud.
  - Jot down any feelings that arose as you read your response.
  - Shake your body free from that perspective.
  - Write about the same challenge from the perspective of why is this happening FOR you.
  - Read your narrative out loud.
  - Jot down your feelings that arose as you read your response.
  - Record your connections and emerging truths.

- Multi-Dimensional Perspective Map

- Divide your paper or page into three columns.
- Label the first column, What do I want from the universe?
- Label the second column, What does the universe want from me?
- Label the third column, What do we (the universe and I) want to do together?
- Soften your eyes and heart and allow the connections to emerge.

Stretching Questions

- What is your capacity to move out of your personal story and into your soul story?
- What determines if you shift stories?
- In what ways might your life be different if you related to the unknown as a place of revelation?

Quotations to Take to Heart

"The power to tell our own story about who we are and who we might become is one of our least acknowledged powers."

Betty Sue Flowers

"It takes only one step and then the frequencies of your soul inform you of the next steps and the next steps. Be aware of what you place your trust in. It matters not what you trust. If there is a wound in your human nature, trusting Big Nature is good medicine."

Big Angel

"There is a vitality, a life-force, an energy, a quickening that is translated through you into action. And because there is only one of you in all time, this expression is unique. And if you block it, it will never exist through any other medium, and be lost. The world will not have it. It is not your business to determine how good it is, nor how valuable, nor how it compares with other expressions. It is your business to keep it yours clearly and directly, to keep the channel open."

Martha Graham

"Your vision should be known to others by how you live, not by what you say." Arjuna Ardagh

"Transformation requires that our attention align with our intention."
Michael Bernard Beckwith

Chapter Five

Befriending Intention

"Like art, manifestation makes soul visible."
David Spangler

A Story about Living With Intention

A thirty-nine year old woman artist arrived during my month long artist retreat. She told me that she had trained for six summers for the Olympics. During supper she shared her frustrations about her failure to get pregnant.

When I asked her if she practiced visualization during the years she trained for the luge competition, she snapped, "We were required to do them. It was a waste of time. I faked it and I hated the time required to picture stuff."

Then she asked why I asked her that question and I explained that I often used visualization techniques to manifest my intentions.

"Making pictures in your mind simply doesn't work. I've proven it," she boasted. "How in the world do you think that visualizing can help me to get pregnant?"

"Perhaps, inviting a baby to join your energy is a softer approach than insisting and commanding," I offered gently. "Perhaps connecting with how much you yearn to be a mother and deserve the opportunity will add another dimension to your desire to be a Mom."

"Anything else?" she asked in a challenging tone.

"I have a sense if you trusted that being a parent is an essential part of your soul's purpose and you sent out an invitation from your soul to the soul of your yet manifested child, you might be surprised."

She said no more and got up and began clearing the table.

I breathed and let go of our conversation feeling content that I had said what was in my heart.

The next day we attended a pottery show and benefit.

We were both drawn to the raffle corner where we admired the 25 pieces of pottery that were donated to the raffle.

"Which three are your favorites?" I asked.

She paused for a moment and pointed to her three selections.

"How about you?" she asked.

I pointed to three different clay creations.

"Are you game for experimenting with visualizing an intention and manifesting it?" I asked.

"Yes, especially if you remind me how to do it."

"You're on," I replied enthusiastically.

I reviewed the manifesting process and emphasized how to connect with how you would feel when you were declared the winner. "It is the principle of over belief" I continued, "believing in something so completely that you are a magnet for that which you plan to manifest."

We practiced. Before we paid for our three raffle tickets, I said,

"All set. Do you feel overflowing with confidence?"

"I'm not sure," she said, falling under self-doubt and the control of her ego.

"Let that thought go. Cancel it. Unless you are 100% confident, your strongest belief will manifest."

"Maybe I will trust myself more when you win one of the three you bet on," she said with a question mark in her voice.

"Nope, manifestation does not work that way. You have to trust yourself first. Besides, I made it my intention to win all three to show you how this process of abundance really works!"

She shrugged her shoulders and said something I did not hear. I knew in advance she would not win and I intuited that she did, too.

I won the three clay beauties that I chose and then gave one away to a ten-year-old girl who had her heart set on the clay doll. After all prosperity is one thing and greed is a story that aligns with ego.

Your resistance to change is likely to reach its peak when significant change is imminent. Choosing faith over doubt and fear aligns you with the energies of manifestation and the power of soul story. Discipline yourself to engage with life as an opportunity, which aligns you with the power of your soul story rather than a struggle, which aligns you with your personal story.

Intentional Thinking

Thoughts are intentions. Every thought and word you speak creates your future. Thoughts take shape and grow when we treat them with silence, intuition, and creativity and then follow through with action. Daily I am surprised when people do not realize the power of their thoughts, especially those ideas voiced with passion.

The old adage, "Be careful what you wish for" is good counsel. I did a double take when I heard friends say laughingly that they hoped that a fire would destroy their building so they could collect the insurance, retire and write books. I wondered why they did not make an intention to clear time and space to write if that was their desire.

Intention Unifies

Transforming our personal story by bridging into our soul story requires attention and intention. Albert Einstein and Niels Bohr discovered that everything in this universe is made up of energy and that includes thoughts. The universe is a unified field and when you state your intention, it is similar to placing your order at a restaurant.

Quantum physics suggests that when you direct your intention, you bring a new course of events into focus while at the same time you can release your existing limited thinking that serves your personal story.

The Elements of Intention

In order to manifest your intention you need to create an energetic match between what you desire in life and your thoughts, feelings and actions. When you shape your intention, include mind, body and spirit. Remember to involve all of your senses, especially your emotions. Feeling is the language that propels intention. Some people can believe in something so passionately that they create an over belief that acts like a mega-magnet that attracts precisely what they are commanding. Both positive expectancy and over belief add energy to intention. The role of imagination is essential in the manifestation process. If you cannot imagine it, you will not manifest it.

Remember to imagine how you will feel when you have manifested your intention. Imagine you have already created that which you desire. How would you feel? For example, you might feel excited, empowered, inspired or even graced. Take the time to reflect on what your intention looks like, feels like, sounds like, tastes like and even smells like.

A Bridging Story Starring Intention

Audrey was on her own for the first time in 64 years. After several false starts, she manifested a large house beside a lake where she planned to jump-start a healing practice that she had abandoned a decade ago in order to devote herself full time to a new relationship. Moments before I walked into her cozy nest, she had learned she was responsible for heat and electricity for the winter. She was panic stricken because the heating bill can be enormous even during a "mild" Maine winter and she had just enough money to pay her monthly rent.

She loved where she was living. The thought of moving away made her heart shrink. Earlier in the week she had returned to her old coffee clatch group and everyone was excited to welcome her back. News carried and former clients had already called her for appointments.

From a soul perspective the scenario was perfect. She had committed herself to re-establishing her healing and teaching practice. Her massage table was set up and her angel pictures hung on the walls. All that was left to do was to print business cards, design workshop brochures to jump-start her prosperity. But first she had to tame the raucous voice of her ego that had almost convinced her that she was in deep trouble.

I refused to support her relapse into being a victim of her personal story. I winked as I said to her, "Imagine how much more light you will be able to channel once you are confident that you can manifest abundance."

When your consciousness changes, the first noticeable difference is how expansive your thinking, feeling, sensitivity and awareness become. You feel more whole than you felt before.

~How would you and your life be different if you believed that
the universe is friendly and eager to support your intention?

~How would your life change if you believed that the transformation that you are seeking is seeking you?

Intention Checklist

Here are some things to consider before commanding your intention:

- Does my intention energize me?
- Does my intention propel me to take an evolutionary leap?
- Is my intention in alignment with my soul purpose?
- Is my intention spacious enough?
- Am I willing to allow grace to add momentum and meaning to my intention?
- Will my manifested intention bless others?

Manifesting the Future in the Present

Manifestation is a process of becoming the person whom you will be when the manifestation succeeds. You do not attract what you want. You attract what you are and what you believe. I consider manifesting to be a sacred act. For me, it is the conscious process of bringing the deepest, purest expression of our life into visible form. Remember to be aware of both parts of intention: what you desire to manifest and who you wish to become. Since you contain all potentials, you will change as a result of successfully manifesting.

If you seriously desire to manifest, you have to be willing to change your previously cherished limiting beliefs that have created your present reality. Remember that the stronger of two opposing feelings will manifest. If you hold the polarities of "I am not sure" and "I am excited to manifest my future" the stronger belief will become your reality. If you wish to track your predominant beliefs and feelings, take a look at what you have called into your life.

For example, after being a full time resident grandmother for nine years, I was not sure if I was ready to step back into the world as a spiritual teacher. However, my excitement about teaching created an irresistible intention. In celebration of my commitment, I printed the title "Cosmic Catalyst" in bold red letters on my business cards and announced my return to teaching on my website: www.heart-soul-healing.com

Positive Thinking Creates Positive Results

The Principle of Manifestation states that what you think, you call into being. If you do not believe that the universe is abundant, creative, and loving, it won't be. Remember the study done at the National Science Foundation that discovered that deep thinkers think around 50,000 thoughts a day. This study also cited that 95% of what people think is negative. Furthermore, they concluded that 90% of what we thought one day is carried over to the next. For some people, saying out loud what they don't want is more familiar than stating a clear intention. Ralph Waldo Emerson, a New England poet who lived almost two hundred years ago, understood the laws of manifestation when he wrote, "Once you have made a decision, the universe conspires to make it happen."

Affirmations Anchor Intentions

Affirmations connect you to the creative energy in the universe. Affirmations need to be clear, firm statements. Claiming and commanding are the energies that shape affirmations. Saying an affirmation in the future tense isn't giving the universe a firm enough command. "I will recover" or "I will enjoy" places you in the future. State your affirmations in present tense. Examples include: I am abundant, I enjoy the universe showering me with abundance, I am healthy, and I delight in being healthy.

Affirmations work best when they are repeated because repetition reinforces belief. I wrap an affirmation up with the phrases "all this and more" and "with ease and grace." Also, remember to request that only the best and highest good be received.

Back to Beliefs

Many of us live our lives based on the outdated beliefs of our parents and grandparents. Unless we inquire about how our inherited beliefs serve us, we stay stuck in out dated limited beliefs. For example, when I lived in England, I was often surprised when someone of my generation showed me a drawer filled with string, elastics, and pieces of cloth that they had saved "just in case" they came under attack in another war. Closer to home, I remember my grandmother telling me I had to work hard, put money in the bank every week, and marry a man who had a good job in order to have a secure future. In retrospect, I am sure she gave her daughter, my mother, the same advice.

~Are you living out some of your parent's or grandparents scarcity patterns, including the belief that you have to work hard to survive?

Some of the common reasons that we do not manifest our intentions include:

- your unconscious has a stronger belief that is opposite of your intention
- you question whether you deserve
- your thoughts, feelings and actions are not in harmony
- your desire is not strong enough
- you have a vow of penance or self sacrifice from another lifetime
- your central nervous system has objections

Befriending Your Central Nervous System

Everything that has ever happened to you is encoded in your central nervous system. Think of it as your internal GPS system. Its primary role is to keep you safe.

Neuroscience tells us that setting an intention "primes" our central nervous system to be on the lookout for whatever supports our intention. You can count on your central nervous system to respond automatically with integrity.

Recall a time when you truly desired to manifest something and no matter how hard you worked to make your plan a reality, nothing happened. The two essential questions to ask your central nervous system with respect and curiosity are:

- What are you feeling
- What do you need?

The dialogue that follows illustrates the value of dialoguing with your safekeeping central nervous system.

Me: Hi, central nervous system. I am curious if I have your support for my intention to manifest financial prosperity?
Central Nervous System: Silence
Me: Let me ask you this: What are you feeling?
Central Nervous System: Ambivalent, to be sure.
Me: I am sorry that you are not sure if you are on my team.
Central Nervous System: You might have saved yourself frustration and disappointment by consulting me before you sent out your intention.
Me: I am curious about your ambivalence and I want to know what I could say or do to encourage you to support my intention.
Central Nervous System: I recall a time when you had lots of money in the bank and you gave it away. Then you over worked to create security for your family. Another time you trusted a partner to invest your money and that led to bankruptcy.
Me: So you don't trust me to make a wise decision about how I will sustain financial abundance? That stuff happened two and three decades ago.
Central Nervous System: Right. And you also have a vow of poverty from a past lifetime. Did you know that?
Me: Nope! But I do know how to release past vows and reclaim my power. I get that I have to win your trust. How about if I promise you that I will keep my financial abundance in the bank? And I will check in with you before making any plans to re-invest it.
Central Nervous System: That is a start.
Me: I appreciate that your job is to do your best to keep me safe. I wouldn't want your job. I also acknowledge that I have a tendency to be impulsive and headstrong.
Central Nervous System: Sigh. You are catching on. Maybe you have grown. I am willing to give you a chance. Know I am nervous and will be watching.
Me: Thank you! I am delighted.

~What is your strongest limiting belief that creates obstacles to manifest your intention?

Begin a dialogue with your central nervous system to explore how best to keep you safe instead of cooperating with your intention to manifest.

I believe that one of the ways we prepare ourselves for future pull is to make space in our consciousness for what we wish to evolve. I had made a vow during my vision quest to design, advertise and teach the seven-month training called Embodying Soul. Saying yes to the person I am becoming meant I consciously re-ordered my priorities and trusted the evolutionary process, my guides and myself. No exceptions.

My first action step in energizing my seven-month intensive was to retire from doing one and two-day workshops. Friends and colleagues thought I was out of my mind, especially in this economy. However, I was determined to manifest more intensive experiences for people. In addition, I trusted that I was in alignment with my soul story, and I was optimistic that the universe would support my expanded intention. I was right. My 2013 seven month Embodied Soul Training filled up and we dove deep. The soul fulfillment that I experienced was a catalyst for me to offer an expanded version of Embodying Soul in 2014. Plans are underway to teach another Embodying Soul training in 2015 and beyond.

The ABC's of Abundance

During my seven-month training, Embodying Soul, many of the participants focused on creating financial prosperity as their primary intention. I encouraged them to expand their definitions of abundance to include being fully conscious and present in the world because I know that our soul recognizes that abundance and freedom are fundamental to our wellbeing.

It is important to understand that money magnifies and amplifies both your positive traits as well as your negative traits. Imagine that your relationship with money mirrors how you feel about yourself.

Remember that your most predominant inner beliefs create your outer reality. Would friends describe you as loving, stingy, cautious, generous, self confident, withholding, judgmental or flourishing?

Next I invited them to think of prosperity as love. The Bible invites us to love one another and serve each other to prosper. What happens when you entertain the thought that your ability to create financial abundance is a mirror of your trust in yourself to manifest your God power into tangible results?

A "Femifestation" Classic

I coined the word "femifestation" one day as I walked on the beach because "femi" means "of the spirit." I smile as I end this chapter with a recent outrageous story of femifestation.

In December 2013, I decided to move to Virginia from Maine to be closer to my daughter and my grandchildren who had moved to Newport News. In preparation for my relocation, I checked for condos or houses for rent in the Newport News area. Nothing appealed to me.

In January, I launched my seven-month training, Embodying Soul, 2014, in Clearwater, Florida. Each morning and evening I walked the beach and every cell in my body was content. Instantly I knew that I yearned to live near the beach. Then I knew that Virginia Beach was my next home. My heart opened the moment I felt the inner resonance of living in Virginia Beach.

Excitement and peace grounded my intention. Immediately, I returned to my room, resumed my Internet search and located a realtor who specialized in renting furnished beach homes. I wrote an email introducing myself and included a video I had just made for my website and two letters of recommendation.

I explained that I wanted a comfortable home that was filled with natural light, a backyard for sculpting, and I wanted to be within walking distance of the beach and The Edgar Cayce Center. Before sending the email off, I visualized myself walking though my new home, smelling the salt air, sitting at my desk writing, sculpting in the backyard, and entertaining family and friends. I breathed in inspiration, creativity, peace and love and welcomed my future self to our new home.

Within thirty minutes, I received a response from Marie Taylor, who said her supervisor handed her my e-mail saying, "I think this is one of your people, Marie." Then she told me she believed she had the perfect home for me.

I asked her, "How do you know that?"

"My intuition," she responded lightly.

I knew she was the perfect realtor for me and also felt the rightness of my decision to move to Virginia Beach, which is about a one-hour drive from my family.

"The only problem is that the house is bigger than what you need and it is more expensive than your budget. But I have already sent your email and your video over to the realtor/owner and I will send you pictures of the beach house which is about twenty feet from the Cayce Center and ten feet from the beach."

I hung up and added more energy to my intention. I imagined dancing in the rooms, lighting candles and incense, and placing bouquets of flowers in the four bedrooms. Then I imagined treating my body to the hot water in the outside shower. I smiled as I thought of how my cats enter a new house—sniffing, lapping, raising their heads and looking around and then rolling over and over.

When I saw the photos of the lime green home, I was filled with the energy of over belief, knowing in advance that the "kiwi" home wanted me as much as I wanted it.

After Trudy Hoff, the realtor/owner, watched my video, she wanted me to rent her house. Together we negotiated a contract I could afford. The process was easy, fun and honored each of us.

Sometimes your original intention to manifest does not work out because your heart is not invested. When your heart is invested, you will know and you can trust your heart to add momentum to your intention.

⊕ Things To Do

- Begin each day by setting a simple, clear intention.
    Make it your intention to give loving attention to yourself or choose to express kindness today. As you walk through your day, appreciate all the opportunities to express or experience loving attention or kindness. Remember that inner kindness counts, too. At day's end, reflect on your experience.
- Draw a line with Prosperity blocked on one end and Prosperity flowing in the other end. Where are you? Then write an action statement and follow through on it within twenty-four hours.
- Repeat the word "Intention" whenever you feel distracted, frustrated or confused. It is an inner reminder to remain focused.

◉ Stretching Questions

What do you desire to transform in your life?
What are your expectations of yourself in relationship to manifesting your intentions?
Who are your manifestation mentors?
What clues are your dreams delivering about manifestation?

♡ Quotations To Take To Heart

"It is in intentionality and will that the human being experiences his identity." Rollo May

"Allowing yourself to believe that everything is possible is another way of expanding your consciousness. Taking action on your inner knowing's activates soul consciousness." Big Angel

"Being intentional in thought, word, and action equals empowerment." Kishori Aird

"Navigating energy through one's intent is the action necessary to shape shift and bring about desired transformation."
Michael Bernard Beckwith

"The rose is itself and the bees come." Swami Sachidananda

Chapter Six

Befriending Meditation

"Meditation is a process by which we go about deepening our attention and awareness, refining them, and putting them to greater practical use in our lives."

Jon Katat-Zinn

Jaiyden's Story

FIVE-YEAR-OLD Jaiyden, the great grandson of Georgia and Dennis Kosciusko, already realizes that meditation feels good. He might even agree that meditation is our true nature.

Jaiyden surprised me a bit before 6:30 this morning, which is the usual time Georgia arrives for our early morning meditation. He announced that she would not be coming over because she was taking care of his little sister.

I asked him if he planned to meditate with me because he had joined us twice. He seemed surprised and pleased.

"Let me run back and see if it's okay," he said and hurried down the thirteen stairs.

He returned minutes later and said he was ready to meditate

As he got to the top stair that leads to the meditation loft, I said,

"Do you remember what we do to get ready?"

"Yep. You put on the light and you plug in the music." Then he headed for his usual sitting spot in the middle of the room.

"That's right. You have a good memory." He beamed and nodded.

"Do you remember what we do next?"

"You light the candle" he said. "Then Amagi lights the smoky stick and then she twirls it round and round," he said proudly.

"Yes," I said, lighting the sage. "Would you like me to smudge you?"
He shook his head.
"And now my Amagi makes the sound with the stick and we close our eyes and are quiet together."
"Would you like to ring the gong to invite us into meditation?"
He smiled and crept over to the round wooden table that had been his great-great grandfather's and made a loud, clear sound. Then we both closed our eyes and settled into silence.

I opened my eyes a few times to be sure he was okay. Both times I noticed his eyes were closed and he looked relaxed and happy. Actually, he looked like an angel.

We both opened our eyes at the same time and smiled at each other.
"Thank you for being here today, Jaiyden"
He nodded.
Then I asked him if he would like to blow out the candle and he nodded again. He watched me closely as he blew out the candle.
"You know, Jaiyden, there is a very wise man from China who believes that if we teach children like you to meditate and feel peaceful inside that in one generation there would be no more wars. And you are doing it."
He smiled and nodded.

I sent out another thanks and a special blessing to all the children like him who will give us a more peaceful and compassionate future.

The Practice of Meditation

Do you believe that it is possible to train your mind to be curious, peaceful and spacious? Meditation is a process of making friends with the mind. The basic experience of meditation combines inner awareness and physical relaxation. Rick Hanson, author of *Buddha's Brain*, describes it this way. "The concentration you gain from meditation takes the spotlight of attention and turns it into a laser beam."

Practicing meditation will teach you how to be conscious of what your mind is doing moment-to-moment and help you disengage from ego and the drama of your personal story. By being aware of your breath, body, and intention you will gradually learn how to let everything be just the way it is moment to moment.

There is no meditation goal—only the process. When we meditate, we are paying attention to awareness itself. Remember that all wanting—especially wanting to be in a certain way is centered on ego and fear.

Here is a journal entry about my relationship with meditation:

Often I find myself rushing to finish tasks or half honoring prearranged commitments in order to meditate. I do not recommend having to catch your breath as a way to begin a relaxing meditation. Another way I get in my own way is by obeying the family rule called Duty. Duty rules when I crowd my life with the voices and demands of many and neglect my own needs for quiet and connection to my inner life.

In silence, there is nothing to do and nobody to take care of or to please. There are no goals or expectations. No need to change or make anything different. I let go of the multiple lists of things to do that I carry around in my head. Absent, too is the need to over give by proving that I am enough. Gradually, I unplug myself from all that makes up my familiar world. Sometimes I distract myself momentarily from the emptiness that silence holds by tracking my inner experiences, cautioning myself to remember fleeting images, key words or prominent sensations. After a few moments, I catch on to my tendency to control and return to surrendering to that which is unfolding within me.

My breathing slows down. I sigh. My body twitches in response. Sometimes I smile or grimace as a childhood memory bubbles to the surface. A few times, I have experienced the whimsicalness inherent in silence. Always, I sense a lightness of being, a deep inner satisfaction and gratefulness for saying Yes" to the "Stop, Look, and Listen," signal within my soul. Silence renews me

Breath as Bridge

Breath is the bridge between the conscious and unconscious mind. Our mind and breath mirror each other. That is the reason I take a conscious breath when I want to feel more deeply or focus more clearly. When we quiet down, we return to our body and our breath.

Here are a few simple techniques that will assist you to be more aware of your breath and move your focus inward.

- Close your eyes. Breathe a sigh. Take three breaths and listen to your mind for one minute.
- When you breathe in, breathe in the whole universe. When you breathe out, breathe out the whole universe.
- Breathe into your heart. Imagine the space in front of you. See the space in back of you. Imagine the space to your right. Imagine the space to your left. Imagine the space above your head and below your head.

Some people prefer to practice a standing or walking meditation rather than a sitting position. I like to alternate between the two postures.

The following standing meditation is a simple way to remain aware of your body as you also attend your breath.

- Hold your arms out in front of you in a rounded position as though embracing a sphere. Keep your eyes open, looking with a soft focus straight ahead into the distance. Breathe naturally.

Another Simple Meditation Practice

I use the following technique to relax my body to prepare for meditation.

- From a standing, sitting, or seated position with your arms naturally extended at your sides, imagine your body has three lines.
- First relax the line from your crown to you coccyx, including your entire spine.
- Next relax the line across your shoulders and arms, down to the fingertips of each hand.
- Then relax the line of your hips and legs all the way down to your toes. Feel each line relaxing and opening.

Meditation As Connection

Our ego has taken on the job of selecting and rejecting experiences.

Isolation and separation are signals that the ego is at work. Meditation enables us to see through our attachments. When we see through to the source of our attachments, they dissolve. Meditation is about making connections. The process involves the skillful use of attention to both your inner and outer worlds.

One of my favorite meditations that fosters connection is the reciprocity meditation, which follows:

- I feel my body. My body feels me.
- I feel my breath. My breath feels me.
- I feel my feelings. My feelings feel me.
- I feel my heart. My heart feels me.
- I feel my guides. My guides feel me.
- I feel the cosmos. The cosmos feels me.

A walking meditation is my favorite way to combine mindfulness and exercise. Virginia Beach is one of my favorite places to indulge myself in an out of doors meditation because I receive instant feedback about my inner balance or disorientation.

As I walk, I focus on something far in the distance like a tanker or a tall tree. Along the way I can count on at least two large groups of seagulls resting on the sand. If I am centered, they do not move as I walk close by. However, if I am not focused, they squawk, disperse, and fly close over my head. I learned how to gauge my inner harmony from a monk who was a beekeeper and never wore a facemask or protection because he learned that if he were centered, the bees would not attack.

The Witnessing Technique

Close your eyes and begin to relax. As you breathe, be aware that each time you inhale you actively pull air in and when you exhale you release the air and relax. Take a few moments and follow this sacred process of reciprocity—breathing in and receiving, releasing and giving back.

If you discover your mind wandering, return your attention gently and lovingly back to the sensations of your breathing. You may wish to silently repeat to yourself: "Breathing in" as you inhale and "Breathing out" as you exhale.

Focus your awareness on the physical environment that surrounds you. Be aware of the sounds. Now bring your awareness to your physical body, the body that supports and sustains you.

Now using your intention and breath, bring your awareness to your mental body, allowing your thoughts to be exactly the way they are. You may choose to label your thoughts when they come up. Be specific. When a thought arises you might say inwardly, "I'm having a thought she is bossy, or having a thought that he is unfair to me, or having a memory of walking on the beach." As you continue to watch your mind, begin to identify the kinds of desires, the "if onlys" and "what if's" that separate you from being present right here and now.

Next using your breath and intention, be aware of your emotions and allow whatever feelings are there to be, without attaching meaning. Name each feeling as it arises. It could be "thinking sadness, sadness, and sadness" until it dissolves and another feeling arises.

Now once again return to your physical body and your breath. Softly open your eyes.

When your mind is free of judgments, stereotypes, interpretations, preferences, and expectations, you are meditating.

The Upanishads, a collection of philosophical texts that form the theoretical basis for the Hindu religion, say that everything in the universe us is meditation.

Noah's Connection Making Story

Noah understands instinctively how to track his inner and outer experiences and to make connections. When he was seven years old, he begged me to take him to Sadhana, a new meditation center in South Portland, Maine. Perhaps I relented and agreed because it had rained five days in a row.

He was excited and he promised to be quiet and listen to anything I said to him. As we went down the stairs to the center, I noticed him examining the brick wall. As we approached the door that led into the main room, he stopped and felt the side of the brick wall. Before I had a chance to ask him what he was doing, he stuck out his tongue and licked a brick.

"Noah, what are you doing? You know it is not healthy to lick bricks."

He turned around and said seriously, "Grandmom, no matter what anyone tells you, these bricks are not real."

"What?" I responded.

"I know because they do not taste the same way as the real bricks that I remember making a long time ago."

Since I was eager to meditate, I did not pursue that story thread. We entered the reception area and removed our shoes. I pointed to a stack of mediation pillows and invited Noah to choose one. Hand in hand we entered the spacious meditation room.

We were alone. Still I whispered, "Remember, Noah, no loud voices, only whispers in here." He nodded. Then I took him to the spot where I usually sat. He shook his head and walked to the center of the room about ten feet away. I reminded him to wait until I had opened my eyes after my meditation before he talked. He nodded again and without another word, he closed his eyes.

Delighted that this was easier than I expected so far, I closed my eyes and opened my heart wider. A familiar sigh arose from the bottom of my belly and I surrendered to the inner silence. When I was finished, I opened my eyes to check on Noah. I was surprised that he had not moved. He remained sitting in his spot, hands on his knees with his thumbs and index fingers connected in a circle. His eyes were closed. Observing meditation etiquette, I did not look at him until he opened his eyes minutes later. Then he wiggled, moved his arms, and stood up. I walked over to meet him and we left the center hand in hand without a word.

When we arrived at my car, I asked, "How was that for you, Noah?"

"Well, Grandmom, the room did not smell like I remember. This place smelled like a hotel. The place I remember smelled like a buttery sweet smell."

I have lived with Noah since he was three months old and I know he has never been inside another meditation center. It was clear to me that his quantum mind had connected to another lifetime.

I asked, "Do you remember where you meditated before."

"In the Himalayas," he said. "Don't you remember, Grandmom, you were there, too."

I shook my head. "No, Noah, I don't remember. Was there anyone else there with us that we know in this life time?"

"My sister was there but she was not called Malia. We called her_____(a very long, peculiar sounding name, which I cannot begin to spell.) And my mother was there, too and we called her _____(another long name that I have no clue how to spell.)

"Noah, what was my name?"

"We called you teacher," he replied.

"Well. Okay, but what was my real name?" I asked.

"We called you teacher," he repeated. Then we both smiled and hugged and agreed that we prefer our relationship better this lifetime because we can laugh, hug and have pillow talks every morning.

This experience reminded me once again that age does not make a sage. Many young people are more awake than their parents or their grandparents. By listening and respecting their remembered experiences, we give them permission to remember all of who they are and they, in turn, teach us to be more open-minded and open hearted.

Our Multi-Faceted Self

The self has many aspects: thinking self, emotional self, functional self that does things, and the witnessing self. It is the witnessing self, or the observing self, that we access in meditation. The witness is that part of your mind that watches whatever is arising, externally and internally, without judging, attaching, or avoiding. It is the part of you that practices non-attachment—the willingness to let things be as they are without trying to make them be the way you would like them to be. Detachment does not mean indifference. It means no expecting.

Witness mind enjoys the experience of existing in British poet John Keats's idea of negative capacity: staying in the unknown and deliberating, leaving questions unanswered. Being content to see what unfolds evokes the witness. When you reside in witness consciousness, you will lose the ego-centered charge that seduces you into believing that your personal story is your only choice.

Benefits of Meditation

- Peace
- Clarity
- Whole brain thinking
- The ability to see though our illusions
- Stability
- Lightness (spaciousness), and well being
- Intuitive insight
- Physical well-being

With sustained practice, meditation leads to calmness and insight.
It gives us the ability to notice the clouds while seeing the sky.
The challenge is to make calmness, inner balance, and clear seeing a part of our daily life. Outflow is a word to describe the way in which the results of meditation spill over into your life.

Still Mind is Mindfulness

Several years ago I attended a talk sponsored by the Lama Foundation, a few miles outside of Taos, New Mexico. The speaker, whose name I have long since forgotten, had recently re-emerged from forty years of silence. His former home was a cave somewhere in the hills of China. He had counted on the kindness of local villagers to feed and clothe him. After four decades of observing silence, his inner guidance ordered him to return to the world to travel and talk to people about what he had learned.

He spoke slowly and softly often looking directly at the woman who served as his translator as if asking her for the right word. His calm manner and his direct gaze touched me. Instinctively, I knew he had some quality that I yearned to embrace. He ended his presentation saying, "Even though you listened to me speak, I want you to know that I continue to experience myself as silent." I believed him and the impact of his statement carries the same power now as it did when I heard him say it many years ago. I wrote it in my journal and I have puzzled about how he managed to do that for years.

Fast-forward twenty years and picture me standing in front of a group of fifty women at a women's leadership conference in Wells, Maine. Months before, I had accepted an invitation from my friend Lou Ann Daly to co-facilitate a conference entitled Women and Power and Women in Community. Two months before the conference I began a rigorous meditation practice that included four hours of silence daily.

Driving four hours to our meeting place, I wondered if I would remember how to resurrect words and be present in a group of women especially since I still felt claimed by solitude and stillness.

My first session was about intution. Meditation strengthens inner listening and my intuition had flourished during my practice. I wanted to teach with my words and also offer an opportunity to teach by my silence. Like the man who had lived in the cave for four decades, I had learned many things within the place of no words.

I stood in front of the group and breathed and looked deeply into the eyes of each woman just as I remember Ram Dass doing during a presentation he made when I was a college student. Another breath and I heard myself saying that I could promise them only two things— depth and delight. Then I took another breath and told the group about my nearly solitary time of silence. My heart opened as my soul reached across time to join the man from China because I experienced that I, too, could speak slowly and softly and still reside in my inner silence.

Eventually, with consistent practice, meditation gives way to compassion and love, which in turn gives rise to connection.

⊕Things You Can Do

- Take time each day to notice the contents of your mind. This act of noticing is one of the most powerful steps to bringing about change. Breathe in a normal rhythm using the phrase, "Peace in" as you inhale and "Peace out" as you exhale.
- Walking Meditation… Walk barefoot with no destination in mind. With each intentional step experience caressing the earth with your foot.
- Nature Meditation.
  Choose or allow yourself to be chosen by some aspect of Nature.
  For example a tree, flower, stream or a cloud.
  Sit with your chosen teacher and become aware of your breath.

Observe your teacher. Open your heart. Then send love to your teacher. In your mind or on paper describe your teacher.

Then for each adjective that you used to describe your nature teacher, substitute "I am."

Visit my website at: www.heart-soul-healing.com and download The Column of Light Meditation by pressing the Giveaway tab.

◯ Stretching Questions

What motivates you to bring moment-to-moment awareness into your daily life?
What does being Present mean to you?
When do you access your inner witness most easily?
What is the role of silence in your life?

♡ Quotations To Take To Heart

"Go within every day and find the inner strength so that the world will not blow your candle out." Katherine Dunham

"As your soul consciousness is activated through practice, it infuses your human consciousness with a lighter frequency. Some call this expanded consciousness. However, from my perspective it is all simply consciousness and you have expanded into it. This experience can happen in meditation or with a kiss."
                              Big Angel

"The art of meditation is the art of shifting the focus of attention to ever-subtle levels, without losing one's grip on the levels left behind."
                              Sri Nisargadatta Maharaja

"Meditation is any activity that keeps the attention pleasantly anchored in the present moment." Joan Borysenko

"Meditation is time spent with God in silence and quiet listening."
                              Marianne Williamson

"When we open ourselves to the silence, there is only the listening."
                              Rainer Maria Rilke

"Just remain in the center watching, and then forget that you are there." Lao-Tzu

Chapter Seven

Befriending Intuition

"Your time is limited, so don't waste it living someone else's life. Don't let the noise of others' opinions drown out your own inner voice. And most important, have the courage to follow your heart and intuition."
Steve Jobs

Crater Lake

I knew something big was up when I had the same intuitive dream three nights in a row. Each time I awoke with the name "Crater Lake" on my mind. When I told a friend of mine who lives in Colorado about the three dreams he said, "I'll be glad to take you there. I know exactly where it is. I've been there several times."

My ego only partially interrupted my intention to visit Crater Lake by trying to convince me that I imagined all of this and besides I would be a burden to my friend. I pinged it and laughed. (I created "Ping"— an acronym for personality issues needing to go.)

The fact that I lived in Maine at the time and Crater Lake was in Oregon and he lived in Colorado did not matter. I recognized the wild calling cards of both intuition and synchronicity. Clearly, this trip was another soul call.

When we arrived at the top of Crater Lake, I got out of the car and my body began trembling and shaking. I clung to the car to avoid falling and my friend held me up. I knew surprises awaited when my hands began shaking as we approached the volcanic lake.

I reminded myself to breathe and remembered that I'd experienced uncontrollable shaking another time—after the birth of my daughter, Kelli Lynne. Clearly, I had no control back then and had none now. Whatever the force was, I knew that I must surrender. So I did. Gradually, my body stopped shaking. I tested my legs and they remembered how to walk. As we approached the lake, I felt overwhelmed with the knowing that I had been here before. I had no specific visual memories, or words, simply a full body intuitive knowing.

Later in the day, I "remembered" how to somersault back and forward in time. Apparently, I had used this technique in past life times to gain information and insight although I had no conscious recall of knowing how to do it before returning to Crater Lake. Several months later I remembered that I had been a spirit guide in the Crater Lake vicinity.

My body memory had opened my heart to another reality before. A few times in England, Scotland, Indonesia, and Egypt, I picked up "energy packets" and came away believing that some times we leave information packets from past life times that we agree to reclaim in another life time.

Tuning Into Our Body

Intuitions register in our body as feelings without any involvement on the part of the mind. Our internal guidance system uses emotion to touch the pain or pleasure part of the brain and lets us know whether we are on track or in danger of making a detour.

You can begin befriending your intuition by recognizing and deciphering your body's signals. Many people use a pendulum to receive intuitive information. When I teach, I remind people that their body is a pendulum and it will give direct responses to yes and no questions. Here's how:

- Say out loud, "My name is (and fill in your correct name.)
- Track how your body supports this truth. You have received a Yes signal.
- Now say out loud, "My name is (and finish the sentence with an incorrect name).
- Track how your body does not support this untrue statement. You have received a No signal.

Your intuitive GPS will deliver information and insight on demand. Your job is to be open, curious, and take action on the information. Remember that your body is your instrument.

I believe that the main purpose of intuition is to provide each of us with the support that we need to fulfill our soul agreements and complete our karmic lessons. Consciously accessing your intuition will connect you to the divine plan that directs your life. My favorite definition of intuition comes from Walter Russell: "Intuition is the language of light through which man and God intercommunicate."

For me, intuition is the silent voice of Spirit. It is the ability to understand or know something immediately and without conscious reasoning. Think of intuition as your connection to your divine potential.

Intuition communicates to us through our imagination. When we deny our imagination, we cut ourselves off from our soul's story and we remain immersed in our small personal stories. Communicating with your intuition is another example of quantum thinking because you connect with information in the quantum field of potentiality. In other words, intuition takes in all the possibilities and directs our energies to make us more purposeful. Michael Lightweaver, author of A *Day of Grace*, summarizes the way of intuition, "When you are fine tuned to this intuitive wave length, that which comes through will be very clear, very precise. Even though it is a reflection of your knowing, it is also coming from a place that is more open, more clear, more fluid then that part of you which normally speaks and is locked into a more limited perspective"

The Ways of Intution

Intuition may come in automatic writing, dreams, blink truths, visions, inner knowing or a feeling of right action. The following automatic writing excerpt from my journal illustrates the power of consciously accessing your intuition.

Being receptive to your intuition is an art form. When you announce your readiness to receive, the universe responds to your unique frequency. That does not necessarily mean you will know everything at once. It does mean, however, that you will be given the perfect amount of insight and additional information will be channeled to you as you grow into your infinite possibilities. Being present to receive inspiration is your part in this collaborative process. Readiness is a frequency— a wavelength. If you believe you are ready, you are.

Silence is a prerequisite for multidimensional knowing. Silence is energy without thoughts.

Since you are in a collaborative relationship with your intuition, treat it is a cherished beloved. Intuition flourishes when it is valued. Each time you access intuition, you tap into the universal mind, which exists in holographic form and often translates as cosmic shorthand.

The choice is forever between form, which is right before your eyes, and essence, which is the unseen energetic blueprint. Here's a story illustrating how we instinctively recognize the difference between form and essence if we take the time to tune into our body's knowing.

A friend called to ask me if I would intuitively check into a waterfront property that he was thinking about buying. He was excited about the prospect of owning this site because it held memories from his childhood.

As he described the property, I was aware of a sharp pain in my belly, which is usually an early warning sign that something is out of alignment. Next, I took a deep clearing breath and asked my guides for a readout on the property.

I saw with my inner eyes two energetic vortexes under the land that were not in harmony. Next, I became aware of an intergenerational history of family feuds. The property looked spectacular and the house appeared more than adequate. However, the land resonated with anger, battles for control, and suffering.

When I told Ed my information, I imagined he would be disappointed. I was surprised when he said, "I felt pain when I stood on the land and I didn't know why other than something felt wrong. I tried to override my feelings but the emotions would not go away."

"Bravo! You were right. Your body spoke truth. I am so glad you listened to your body." Then he cleared his throat and admitted that he had made a good will offer on the land in spite of his inner knowing that his soul did not support getting involved with that property. You betray yourself when you receive intuitive information and act against it, repress it or deny it.

It is possible to turn around negative energies and redirect negative vortexes and even heal the land of intergenerational conflicts and greed. However, why not scout out a property that resonates with Essence?

Intuition or Mind Chatter?

Intuition can be understood as the mind turning in on itself and understanding the result of processes that took place outside of our normal awareness. When we open up to our intuition, we get very different results. Shifting out of a thinking mode into a calm, meditative state is one way to invite your intuition. Remember to detach from preferences and what you know to be true and possible. Then invite your intuition to gift you with possibilities and alternate realities. The following list illustrates the difference between personality and intuition:

Personality	Intuition
Trying Hard	Ease
Control Based	Love based
Restrictive	Expansive
Closed	Open ended

These questions will help you to distinguish between intuition and mind chatter or magical thinking:

- Is the information grounded in love?
- Does this information add to your potential?
- Does the information have a sense of truth and rightness?
- Does the information move you closer to your future self?

Be confident that you have accessed your intuition if you responded yes to the questions listed above.

Clear intuitive guidance directs you with love and compassion. Frances F. Vaughan, author of *Awakening Intuition,* puts it this way, "With intuitive insight comes self-acceptance, compassion and love." The movement is from information to guidance to wisdom.

Remember we are always in a relationship with our intuition. As we nurture and value our inner guidance, the relationship becomes more intimate and more immense. In the process of befriending your intuition, expect to confront any forms of self-deception that your ego creates and maintains. Messages from your ego or intellect tend to be based on thoughts of scarcity, guilt, or fear. Genuine inner guidance makes you feel open, expansive, and balanced.

Road Blocks to Intuition

- Negative beliefs
- Low self-esteem
- Rigid thinking
- Inability to relax
- Distrust of the unknown
- Need to control
- Over dependency on linear thinking
- Failure to act on intuitive insight

Another Belief Inventory

Unexamined family beliefs can create limitations that inhibit our intuition. For example, reflect on your mother and father's attitudes about intuition. Then take a breath and make it your intention to identify your grandparents' attitudes about intution. Shake your body free of any limiting or toxic beliefs. When you befriend your intuition, you may need to surrender cherished beliefs about what you know and do not know as well as who you are.

Neither our parents, nor our grandparents, or anyone else can teach us or model for us what they did not acknowledge or value. In fact, nobody can validate you for what you are unwilling to claim yourself. For example, I was born intuitive. Neither of my parents believed in intuition. Their reality, like so many people who survived the depression, was based on what they could see and touch.

When I was in my fifties, my grandmother whispered to me one summer evening that her paternal grandmother read tea leaves and brought the Ouija Board into the parlor every Saturday night and led séances! Who knows why that story remained a family secret for generations? I cried when she told me that story because for the first time I knew I had an intuitive woman in my lineage.

Follow Through As Feedback For Intuition

One day in an airport waiting area I consulted my intuition in the midst of a stressful situation. A young boy, who was about 8 years old, held everyone's attention in terminal B at the airport in North Carolina. He was loud and sassy to his mother. I watched as he angrily shook his hands close to her face. She smiled, kept her voice low and looked calm. Initially, I was impressed with her patience. Then he screamed and poked his fists about two inches from her face.

I was afraid that he would hit her. Like everyone else who watched, I did nothing for a few seconds. Then I closed my eyes and asked my intuition for guidance. Instantly, I saw a moving picture of me approaching the mother and son and asking for permission to hold the boy's hand while I surrounded both of them with love.

When I opened my eyes to reorient myself, I did not walk the ten feet that separated us. I was afraid that I might look weird or seem arrogant. Instead I remained seated and energetically sent them love and calmness. I was not happy with myself because I know that acting on inner guidance gives feedback to my intuition that I received the information and valued it enough to take action. Moments later, he did back off and lowered his voice.

Sometimes bridging personal stories in favor of soul story is as simple as choosing between our scared self and our capable self. Intuition aligns with capable self. Although my ego scored temporarily, I made a commitment to myself to take action on my guidance in the future—even if I am uncomfortable because others are watching. I have learned through painful experience that the more I do not take action on the intuitive guidance that I received, the more I begin to fear my inner voice and vision.

After the incident, I thought about negative capability which is a theory developed by John Keats, a British poet, who wrote about the capacity to be in uncertainties, mysteries, and doubts without any irritable reaching after fact and reason. If intuition is to emerge as knowledge without comprehension, you must be able to tolerate that lack of mental clarity. If intuition takes time to gestate, you must be prepared to wait, to resist the desire to end the discomfort and confusion by forcing an answer or understanding. The willingness to let things be as they are, rather than trying to make them be the way you would like them to be allows intuition to emerge.

Guidance From my Guides

My guides excel at channeling information about intuition.

Soft focus, soft touch, soft heart. Softness is an attribute of your soul, which connects you to your intuition. Softness is not the same as gullibility. Discernment is present within softness. It is the energy of softness that readies a heart to remember its lightness. It is, indeed, lightness of your Being that motivates you to rid your consciousness of outdated beliefs, past dysfunctional habits, and shadow aspects in order to be more present for your soul story

On another day my guides dropped in and channeled this:

A soft focus invites a deeper awareness and a reverence for the process of evolving beyond your personal story. Your reality is entrained to an expanded, multi-dimensional consciousness. Each time you consciously relax, you are there. It is not a journey, merely a readjustment, and an inner attunement. With practice, the process becomes seamless.

Lauren Artress, author of *Walking A Sacred Path*, reminds us, "One of the things we forget most easily is how to ask for help from the Divine." In my workshops I challenge people to consider that their intuition is a highly paid consultant and each time they fail to consult it, they have to write a check to their least favorite charity.

This automatic writing excerpt from my journals illustrates how intentionally tuning into your intuition brings clarity as well as a way out of obedience to your personal story:

Me: Thank you for treating me with guidance about the dance between will, trust and surrender. My primary question: Is trusting the same as surrender?

Guides: It depends. At times you are invited to trust that all is in alignment with your Highest Good. If you are convinced that you know what is best, then surrender is the learning. Letting go of a preferred outcome is a form of surrender.

Me: At times I have prided myself on my will, which I now appreciate was the polarity of trusting, certainly of surrender.

Guides: As you learn to attune to higher will and then universal will, letting go is easier. Breathe. Be easy. Understand that growth and evolution are incremental. Cooperation accelerates the process. In time (laughter) the

> *choice for transcendent unity becomes habitual because it delights and unifies all.*

Me: I deeply desire to live my life from that perspective. I yearn to merge with the transcendent—not to bypass ordinary reality, but as a soul seeking unity.

Guide: *Once you have been swept into the dynamics of grace, bliss beckons. That is the path of a mystic. Nothing else fulfills. Please appreciate that both trust and surrender empower.*

Catalysts for Intuition

- Relaxed awareness
- Single minded focus
- An attitude of non-attachment
- An openness to wonder
- An ability to suspend judgment
- An irresistible energy field

~Imagine for a few minutes who you would be if you truly trusted your intuition to guide you.

Engaging Your Intuition

Albert Einstein wrote, "Intuition does not come to the unprepared mind." The quality of our intuition depends mainly on our state of consciousness. Here are the steps to consciously accessing your intuition.

- Create an irresistible field of energy by remembering people you love deeply and people who love you deeply. Expand your awareness to appreciate times when you experienced joy. Now breathe in the remembered energy of places that resonate with beauty and sacredness to you.
- Move your attention and intention to your high heart, the energy center about two inches above your human heart that some people refer to as spiritual heart.
- Breathe in peace as you inhale and breathe out peace as you exhale.
- Imagine that you have roots extending from the bottom of your feet

- and send your roots down deep into the earth. Breathe the earth energy into your feet, legs and into your belly,
- Savor the sensations of groundedness and stability.
- Bring your attention and breath to the top of your head. Imagine you have an opening in the center of your head. Send out your cosmic roots and connect with the heart of the cosmos.
- Breathe in the unconditional love through the opening in your head, down your face, into your high heart.
- Savor the experience of spaciousness.
- Be aware of the merging of universal energy and earth energy in your body.
- Smile.
- Imagine two pathways or antennae that extend from your ears. Label one "incoming information" and label the other "outgoing gratitude."
- Affirm that you are delighted to channel your inner wisdom.
- Write or type Thank you for the guidance about how (I can be even more receptive to my intuition.)
- If you experience a pause in the flow of energy, smile and write Thank you, thank you, thank you until you catch up with the transmission.

My Guides Speak Out

Sometimes I feel like a cosmic secretary and I giggle and acknowledge that I signed on for this job. Give yourself permission to initiate a dialogue with your intuition, guides and God. After all, your relationship with your intuition is reciprocal. Stay tuned as information transforms to wisdom and revelation as you deepen your trust of yourself, your intuition, and the evolutionary process.

Here is an excerpt from my journals of intentionally dialoguing with my intuition.

Me: Thank you for information about anything I need to be aware of right now in my life.
Guides: Dear One, We are here.

Me: Yes, and I appreciate your guidance.
Guides: Much is being asked and expected of you by us as well as your human counterparts.
Me: I do feel more open, more energetic and more compassionate. I enjoy being of loving service.
Guides: *Yes, for that is the way of the Divine. Remember you are a spark of the Divine.*
Me: Thank you.
Guides: *Your time has come. Moving from self-confidence to spiritual confidence is your theme for the coming months. Reflecting on what you chose to leave behind and whom you choose to commit yourself to become is also part of the process. Creative generosity energizes you. Sculpt, write, dance, rattle, and make love. For all these forms will deepen your confidence and trust.*
Me: Sigh! I had a hunch that was what was happening.
Guides: *All that and more!*

Be aware that as your relationship with your intuition grows, information may arrive at all times of the day and night. Sometimes guides seem to ignore our human need for sleep. Here is where imagination comes in. I announced to my guides that I would leave my energetic answering machine on all night while I sleep and in the morning I would transcribe all the night's messages. It worked. They felt acknowledged and I felt rested.

I admit to having a history of resisting and rebelling when someone tells me what to do. However, I have learned how to ask for and accept guidance from my intuition. In fact, I enjoy inviting my guides to remind me of what is possible. Here is another example.

Me: What is my work this lifetime?
Guides: *Your work is to express yourself heartfully and outrageously.*
Your work is to remind yourself that you have the courage to complete.
Your work is to teach and challenge others how to express their truths.
Your work is to communicate your own experience, expertise, wisdom and grace.

Meeting Big Angel

The circumstances surrounding my initial encounter with Big Angel were humorous. Picture this scene. I was in the middle of giving a workshop on Soul Empowerment at Leapin Lizard's, a metaphysical bookstore in Portland, Maine and I took a bathroom break. You may not wish to picture me sitting on the toilet but that is when Big Angel announced his name and his presence to me. I distinctly heard a voice and it was definitely male. I rushed to pull my pants up while he asked for my permission to teach the group about how to align with future self. I was attached to introducing the new concepts that I had been working with for several months, but I took a deep breath and thought to myself, "Ah! An angel with an agenda."

Then I remembered that all the angels I have met had an agenda. My curiosity overcame my insistence on leading the exercise myself. When Big Angel asked to merge with my human energies in order to lead the exercise, I agreed.

I recognized the quickening of my energy and the lightness in my head as a sign of an angel's arrival because I remembered channeling The Angel of Findhorn during the fifteenth anniversary party in Forres, Scotland. I joked to friends that I was becoming the queen of surrender. Allowing another to occupy my consciousness and my body felt like the ultimate challenge. However, learning how to express in linear words the Big, Bold, Beautiful and Bright Truths that Big Angel channeled through me felt even bigger.

Although I was aware that my energy felt quickened, my cheeks were flushed, and I felt like I was having a hot flash from inside out, none of the participants guessed Big Angel was their instructor. Perhaps because Big Angel had merged into my high heart, I looked normal. He remained invisible. My mouth opened and Big Angel and I walked the participants through the multi-dimensional exercise. Although I spoke the words that led the participants through the merging with future-self exercise, I was in awe of the simple yet profound process. It was way beyond what I had experienced personally or prepared for the group.

Over time I discovered that one way to play with the angels was to embrace my radiance. High beam living and loving is how I source and express my authentic power and align with the Divine.

Angels are our allies and they have no understanding of our human tendency to settle for survival rather than fully flourishing. At all times they mirror our divinity and invite us to open to our divine potential. They excel at reflecting a future memory of being all that we can be, which includes the unfolding and claiming of our divine potential which brings boundless joy to them.

Big Angel enjoyed enlightening me. His definition of enlightenment is bringing in more light. Here are a few of the succinct teachings of Big Angel:

I am one of the interdimensionals. I serve many dimensions. My assignment is to remind you of the Truth and Beauty that live within each of you.

Allowing yourself to believe that everything is possible is another way of expanding your consciousness. Taking action on your inner knowing's activates soul consciousness.

You invite by your light. Your light, your laughter, your stories and your compassion attract others. Your love invites others to align more deeply while you hold the frequency of the future. Once a person has a taste of their inner sovereignty returning to the restricted, familiar ways has little appeal.

Many are the ways to attract us: silence, intention, beauty, fragrance, curiosity about past lifetime or future time beyond this moment, reading the words of the prophets and mystics, creative acts, love, writing without thought, joy, kindness, living in your heart and prayers.

From that April day in 2012, until September, 2013 Big Angel and I were a team. Big Angel disappeared without warning when Mary appeared for the second time in my life. I have no idea how that is decided except I have had lots of experience with my guides coming and going. My sense was Big Angel was on a special assignment with me. In workshops I include a guide review process and participants ascertain if their present guides are awaiting re-assignment and if they are we do a send off and gratitude ritual and we also welcome new guides.

Intuitive Dreaming

Intuition also manifests through dreams. Each time we remember and examine a dream, we have a picture of our unconscious. Symbolism is the natural language of dreams. Dreams can be either psychological or psychic. Psychic dreams offer guidance. When Einstein wrote about the principle of relativity, he did so in a dream state. "In order to complete the law of relativity," he said, "I have to sleep in the right side of my brain."

Remember that in dream life the brain is still outside of the intellect's control. That is why it is possible to be in two different places within a dream. That makes no sense in ordinary reality, but perfect sense in quantum reality.

Working with our intuitive dreams allows us to collaborate with our unconscious. The following dream and subsequent work illustrate some of the possibilities.

A loud sound like something breaking interrupted a dream I was having. I laid still thinking that if I did not move, I would remember the remnants of the dream well enough to record it in my journal. Here's what I remembered:

I am standing in the middle of a circle of tall pine trees. I am dressed in a long, white flowing dress with a rainbow colored shawl around my shoulders. My feet are bare and my toes are decorated with pink iridescent nail polish. Seven tapered candles hung from tree branches. I have the sense that a commitment ritual was about to take place.

Then in present time I crawled out of bed and got a glass of water. The clock said 3:01. Once under the covers, again, I reached for my journal in hopes that more pieces of the dream would come together.

I was surprised when my intuition broke through before I had the chance to apply the following guidelines and dance the dream awake.

> *Guides: It is time to choose yourself. Let go of your wish to be chosen by another. Be responsible. Choose yourself.*
> Me: What does that mean exactly?
> *Guides: You were about to make the vow of choosing yourself in the dream. It is your next evolutionary step.*
> Me: I still don't understand how choosing myself will serve me?
> *Guides: That is because you have never done it before. Choosing yourself allows you to reside in the witness place of your consciousness. No matter*

> *what happens, you will no longer be driven by the false expectation that someone will love you more than you love yourself. Choosing yourself means you are the source of your own love. Your destiny is to be open hearted.*
>
> Me: I understand. I have a strong sense that this is connected to a relationship that I imagined would grow into a conscious, loving relationship.
>
> *Guides: Dancing the dream awake means turning dreams into physical realities.*

Before dawn, I put on a long sleeved white dress, tossed a multi-colored shawl across my shoulders, grabbed seven candles, a lighter, and walked to the pine grove. My four cats followed. After lighting the candles, saying a prayer, and inviting in the energy from the six directions (north, south, east west, above and below), I knew I was ready to make my covenant.

I vowed to love myself in ways I wished another would cherish me.
I vowed to reclaim my sovereignty.
I vowed to be open to my wisdom voice.

Choosing myself felt like a marriage vow. I am reminded of a Rumi line, "To find the beloved, you must become the beloved."

Before I continue with the after effects of the intuitive dream, here are some guidelines for making purposeful meaning from intuitive dreams:

- Write the dream in the present tense as if it were happening right now.
- Circle all the action verbs. What kind of movement does the dream portray?
- Underline words or concepts that intrigue you.
- Write about the deeper meanings of the words or concepts you underlined.
- Highlight any polarities. What do the splits signify to you?
- Read the dream out loud. Record your feeling response to the dream on a separate line.

- Write a dialogue with the dream. Example: Dream, what do you most want me to know?
- Create a dialogue between people, objects and events in your dream.
- Name the dream and put the title above the first line of the dream.
- Date the dream.
- Make a commitment to take action on one part of the dream.

Often guidance will come and when you act upon the information, more will become available. However, you may receive one piece of information at a time. When you take action, you send feedback to your intuition that you received the information. Your intuition responds to your trust by giving you more information.

Completing the ritual of choosing myself was the initial invitation. Although my agreement made no sense to my mind, my heart sensed the importance. I had been looking forward to being with a soul friend for a week and deepening our relationship. We both agreed it was time. Being in my heart with my friend was familiar so I was puzzled about how the agreement to choose myself fit in with my upcoming visit. I was not prepared for the intensity of the learning curve.

My friend had recently returned from a trip aboard with another woman and he remained energetically bonded with her throughout my visit. I was surprised and disappointed. Yet because of the ritual of choosing myself, I remained centered in my heart because that is who I am. No exceptions.

One of the tasks of a karmic relationship is completing the karmic history from an open heart. I asked myself several times during the week, "Where is the opportunity for evolutionary growth in my relationship?" Then I inquired from an opened hearted place, "What is my part in the unfolding drama?" reminding myself that I always have responsibility for co-creating events in my life.

If I had not made the vow to choose myself, I would have gotten angry, or even closed down my heart. This event felt like one of those final exam times that offer opportunities to embrace our authentic Self. From an open heart I appreciated my role in the creation of the event that was perfectly orchestrated for the benefit of the well being of all.

I believe that we can all arrive at the place where there is little or no transition between us speaking and our intuition or higher self communicating.

Befriending Intuition

It is time to move from intuitive guidance into divine revelation. Here is my shorter version of consciously accessing my intuition.

- Surround every cell in your body with love.
- Breathe in the love of the universe.
- Repeat to yourself, I am love loving.

Keeping a journal about your intuitive progress builds confidence. Remember to record dreams that contain intuitive elements. Then deepen your process by dancing your dream awake.

⊕ Things To Do

Ask your intuition to introduce two of your gifts and talents that are waiting to emerge.

Reflect and then write about what you need from your intuition. Then ask your intuition what it needs from you.

⊙ Stretching Questions

What situations or people spark your intuition?
Do you consult your intuition to gain information in relationship to personal story, soul story, none or both?
When do you count on your intuition?
When was the most recent time you followed your intuition?
When has your intuition shown up in your dreams?

♡ Quotations To Take To Heart

"Awakening intuition enables one to see the choices available."
                                        Frances Vaughan

"Your intuition effaces ego." Big Angel

"Our soul's hunger for the lost connection to our intuitive nature expresses through myths, dreams, stories, and images. We long for a creative, symbolic process that nurtures our spiritual nature, that feeds our soul." Lauren Artress

"Believe it only if you have explored it in your own heart, mind, and body and found it to be true." Buddha

"Intuition is less about divining the future than it is about entering more authentically into the present. It often evades conscious recognition." Joan Borysenko

"Intuition is really a sudden immersion of the soul into the universal current of life." Paulo Coehllo

In the next chapter you will discover how imagination links intuition and creativity. Andrew Weil, author of *The Natural Mind*, summarizes the connection: "The history of science makes clear that the greatest advancements in man's understanding of the universe are made by intuitive leaps at the frontiers of knowledge, not by intellectual walks along well traveled paths."

Chapter Eight

Befriending Creativity

"The mysterious dance of our lives is a partnership between our free creativity and the incessant lure of the divine."
Mark Riddell

CREATIVITY, intuition, and healing co-exist for me. I was called to sculpting more than two decades ago when my friend Sarah submitted her fragile body to chemotherapy and radiation. I was determined to give her something she could hold in her hands during her treatments. I was startled when the idea of making her something from stone popped into my head.

When I picked up my first piece of alabaster, I stared at the three-pound rock and hyperventilated! Every negative statement that I had swallowed since childhood about my inability to make art flooded me. Then I cried. Without warning I sensed a strong current of energy that seemed to emanate from the stone. Without thinking, I responded to the dismissive voices inside my head and the inviting energy from the stone, by shrieking, "I will make something healing for Sarah to hold."

I wish I could write that sculpting was easy. I can't. I wish I could say that I was overwhelmed with inspiration and grace from the stone. I can't. I wish I could brag that I never again doubted that I was creative. I can't. Looking back, all I knew was that I was passionate about creating a form that Sarah could hold in her two hands to remind her that she was whole in spite of the potential danger and benefits of chemotherapy. Five days later I gave Sarah a small polished figure of a woman in the child's yoga position. She smiled at me, unable to speak because of the ventilator in her mouth. I watched as she caressed the shiny figure and turned her over and over. She nodded her head and we both cried.

Almost three decades later, I continue to be a student of stone, intuition and healing. Even now I hold the stone close to my heart before I pick up a diamond-studded file. Then I lift it close to my ear in case this is the stone that will introduce me to its music. Next I caress the stone and turn it over and over studying the texture, the angles and the way light enters. If the stone is not too big, I put it under my pillow and dream with it. I invite my intuition and nature to inspire me.

Befriending my unique form of creative self-expression awakens my yearning for wholeness. Each time I do a soul reading, I am in touch with each person's unique beauty as well as each individual's unique form or forms of creative expression. During the past thirty-five years of offering soul readings, I have learned that creative self-expression is as spacious as stars in the sky.

> As an artist I enter the mystery each time I interact with stone or clay.
> As an artist I intentionally invite the elements of earth, water, air and fire to have their way with me.
> As an artist I ground myself in my body, my instincts, and my intuition as I await inspiration.
> As an artist, I intentionally use my hands as extensions of my heart.
> As an artist, I awaken to unseen connections and invite my muse and the lineage of artists to illuminate my creation.

The Pregnant Nun Sculpture

Creating art is one way I integrate unfinished personal business and heal past wounds. It does not matter if the unresolved issues are connected to my recent lifetime or a past lifetime. When I allow my hands to be an extension of my heart, I connect with a field of infinite possibilities. The following saga illustrates how my creativity and healing intertwined (eventually).

The lopsided stone sat on my bureau for almost two years. It was the last thing I saw before I surrendered to sleep and the first thing I saw as I greeted the morning. I circled the stone for months sensing the sculpture within the stone that waited for me. The name, The Pregnant Nun, shouted to me from the ten pound white alabaster stone weeks before I had a clue about the stone's destiny.

Some days I filed for hours uncertain who or what might emerge from the stone. Eventually two curves that looked vaguely like mounds and gradually transformed into breasts faced me. The gigantic breasts reminded me of the stone sculptures of the ancient Paleolithic Goddesses.

Sexuality has shadowed me this lifetime. I remember the past lifetime when I was the pregnant nun—the passion, devotion, excitement, soul searching, shame and death. As a pregnant nun in the early 1200's, I lived on the ancient island of Iona in the Inner Hebrides off the western coast of Scotland. I explored the separate calls of spirituality and sexuality and was murdered because my lover, a priest, was not able to reconcile his love for me with his vows of celibacy.

In July 2012, I brought the unfinished stone nun to my month long artist retreat. I placed her carefully on a circular turn style in my studio. She beckoned as I learned to play with clay early in the morning. I returned to work with her in the afternoon. Gradually, I figured out how to form a belly that bulged with pregnancy, but the proportions were wrong. The breasts were massive and the tummy was too small. Plus, the cone shaped head looked like an alien. I struggled with her head for weeks. It tilted the wrong way. Then it was too big. Each time I adjusted her head, I also had to adjust her swollen breasts and protruding belly. Then I realized that her spine was no longer in alignment with her new head.

I do not enjoy attending to small details, whether in writing, designing workshops or sculpting. I fantasized about running away and floating in the nearby pond, inviting the sun to melt away my frustrations. In the end, I lopped her head off (I do not recommend this technique) and I was delighted when the thick upper part of her back also separated. Ultimately, I chose to leave her upper back raw and unsanded.

My persistent critical voice chided "How can you possibly think you can sculpt a nude woman's pregnant body when you have never had an art lesson or an anatomy class?" No matter how loud my light dimming voice screamed, my soul would not permit me to abandon her or myself. I understood from a deep place within myself that this piece held both freedom and healing for me.

I stood for hours in front of my bathroom mirror examining the contours and angles of my breasts and how they were attached to my body. I twisted and turned my body and tried to remember how my belly looked when I was pregnant. Later I joked with my friend Ed that I bet I was as fascinated with breasts as most men are. He quipped, "I don't think so, Rosie."

About two weeks into my retreat, I asked Squidge Davis, my pottery teacher, to help me. She picked up the stone, studied it, ran her hands over the different textures, caressed it from all sides, and said without judgment, "Hmmm, she has no arms. That is why she looks unbalanced."

I was stunned. I could not believe I had missed that important detail. Then I almost gave up again, because I knew, unlike clay, I could not add arms to stone. In the midst of my frustration, my heart opened up. I realized the pregnant nun without arms was perfect. This unfinished woman could not reach out for support because she had no arms.

At that moment, I decided to relate to sculpting as my spiritual practice. I reminded myself to breathe, file with awareness, let go of attachments, release blame, judgment, and be curious—without expecting anything. Each time I considered giving up, I replaced resignation with breath and filed deeper. At night, my dreams opened up and showed me how to look at the emerging woman from all directions before I picked up a file.

In April, the unfinished alabaster nun flew with me to New Mexico, my soul's home. I knew my sculptor friend Jonna, would remind me how to round her too square belly. "File deeper," she laughed, and told me to get rid of more stone. I breathed and said, "Oh, I get it, less is more." We laughed. Then I centered myself in my belly and used my strong right arm to penetrate the stone. White dust covered my face and I continued to file. One hour flew by. The pregnant nun emerged in her final form.

I was aware that a two-year re-claiming project was close to completion. I took a breath and reminded myself to savor this precious moment. The part of me that longed to have the sculpture completed was impatient and I assured her that I was aware that there was still work to do. However, the hard labor was over. For a few minutes I simply wished to honor the stone and myself before sanding, sealing and polishing it.

Next, I decided to create a flat surface at the bottom of her body in case I decided to mount her on a stone base. Then I quickly let that idea go when I sensed that she desired to be held—not confined to a base.

Upon returning to Maine, I visited Squidge. I'd not seen her for eight months. I brought the pregnant nun sculpture with me. I was eager for Squidge to see the completed woman. Once again, she examined her thoroughly in the sunlight and complimented me on the beauty and the simplicity of the sculpture.

She whispered, "She is perfect, Rosie. She is not complete until she is held in your hands."

"Yes," I replied softly, surprising myself, "I plan to use her as a speaking vessel in my workshops. She is my version of the Native American talking stick that is passed from person to person as they speak in a circle. She is a symbol of the deep feminine."

"Yes," we said in unison.

I have yearned to live in the sacredness of love my whole life. Being in a conscious, loving relationship is part of my soul purpose. By bringing the pregnant nun into form, I have re-connected to my body, my sexuality, my sacredness and my wholeness. My gifts to the nun are freedom to choose, play, curiosity, and creativity. Her gift to me is blessings of body and spirit. Together we heal.

At its deepest heart, creativity is meant to serve and evoke beauty. I have a passion for beauty. I challenge myself to encounter beauty daily. Beholding beauty nurtures my soul as much as creating beauty. John O' Donahue, author of *Beauty*, speaks to my heart when he writes, "We were created to be creators." If I forget or become too busy, I can always return to my journals and read about my visits with beauty when I am in need of inspiration. Here is an excerpt from one of my journals that describes a memorable encounter with beauty.

Nature's Beauty

The drive on 95 between Bangor and Portland, Maine is crowded with tall pine and birch trees. There is one spot that always fills me with awe and reminds me to slow down and appreciate the natural beauty that surrounds me. Today, January 10th, 2014, the ice covered trees sparkled in the sunlight and I pulled over to the side of the road in order to savor the sight. The sun created light sparkles everywhere. My heart was happy. Then I spotted the revolving blue lights of a police car that had pulled up in back of me.

The office tapped at my window. Since it was 20 degrees below zero, I invited him to sit next to me in my warm car.

"Anything wrong, Ma'am?" he asked in an official voice.

"No," I replied honestly.

"Then why are you parked in the break down lane?" he inquired, while looking me directly in the eyes.

"I wanted to get a closer look at the trees and how beautifully the sun is lighting them," I said honestly. "And I did not want to endanger myself or anyone else by driving."

"What do you do?" he asked politely.

I ran over the roles I play in my mind—cosmic catalyst, teacher, grandmother, artist, and writer and decided that writer might be the safest.

"I write," I said without further explanation.

He smiled and said, "That explains it. My mother is a poet and she would stop her car in a break down lane to look at trees, too." Then he opened a file and pulled out a piece of paper. I thought he might be about to give me a ticket. Instead he wrote the name and telephone number of his mother because he thought we might enjoy talking about beauty and the written word.

Then he said he would follow me for a few miles, "just in case you need to stop again because of a beauty seizure" and then he jumped out of my car.

Creative Thinking

Creative thinking involves making the familiar strange and the strange familiar and feels as natural as breathing to me. I taught creative process at the Creative Problem Solving Institute in Buffalo, New York, for more than three decades. One of the ways to jump start your thinking is beginning a problem solving challenge by asking, "In what ways might I… finishing with what you want to create. In my case it's often "In what ways may I be more present for my creativity?" I enjoyed the stimulating practice of brainstorming and introducing the six step Osborne-Parnes creative problem solving model to others. However, I longed to create with my hands as well as my mind. I sensed that my intuition was ready to serve me and awaited a hands-on experience. The idea of making art delighted my mind, body, and soul.

Beginning at The Beginning

If you were conditioned to believe that you have to get your life in order before you express yourself creatively, I suggest that you banish that belief because you may be setting yourself up for not expressing yourself at all. Too many of us were raised with this restricting belief: Work before play.

I know from experience that when I become too busy or when I stray too far from my imagination, I cut myself off from my soul's story. Furthermore, I have observed that people who describe themselves as creative tend to fall into depression more than others who do not value their unique form of creative expression.

Creative inspiration visits when I embody some form of creativity and depression is a signal that my spirit suffers from creative ennui. For me, embodying my creativity is a basic need, as essential as fresh water, nutritious food and collaborative sex. That is why I indulge in at least one form of creative expression each day. Writing, doing soul readings, designing workshops, sculpting and being with my grandchildren are synonyms for creativity for me.

Here are some questions designed to jump start your unique form of creative self expression:

- What did you learn from your parents and grandparents about limiting or expanding your unique form of creative self-expression?
- Who were your models for creativity in childhood?
- In what ways was your self-expression thwarted as a child?
- In what ways did you protect your parents by toning down your self-expression?
- In what ways are you still influenced by that decision to tone down?
- What does your soul yearn to express?

My Creative Process: Stone and Clay

Each time before I walk into my studio, I invite my four-year-old inner little girl, Rosalie Ann, to accompany me. Growing up, she felt isolated from her creativity. Yet I have learned she has amazing instincts and is an expert about rhythms. She lets me know when I am not paying attention to my body and jumping ahead of myself and she also cheers when I embrace my own rhythms of rest, activity and stillness. I remind her each time we are together how much I love her and cherish her presence in my studio. We are a team. I am putting into practice William Thierry's belief, "The art of arts is the art of love."

In order to create art I have to set my mind aside along with my tendency to overachieve and then override my limiting belief that I know nothing about artistic creativity. My ego is like the big, bad wolf in Little Red Riding Hood. It is vigilant and devours any pulls to engage in creative expression. My inner wolf values productivity and shuns innovation as "child's play" and chides me to be an adult. Shame is Wolf's favorite ploy. He ran my life for decades and remains alive in my consciousness and now I use my creativity to override his voice.

Pythagoras, a Greek philosopher and mathematician, believed that stones were frozen music. I have never heard a stone sing, but I have learned valuable lessons from stones. I am deeply aware that my first cut with the file will forever change the stone's structure. I hold my breath when I file for the first time. Then I take a breath, listen and watch, hoping for a response from the stone. Once again I study the angles and wait to see if the stone will call me into a collaborative relationship.

Often I file too softly at first. I am cautious. I don't want to make a mistake. I let go of the first several forms that I imagine the stone can become in favor of being curious. Then I put the stone down and stand back a few feet and gaze at it and remind myself that each time I let go of a perspective, I create space for more forms to emerge.

Stone teaches me about persistence and vulnerability. I walk away when I get frustrated. Then the negative refrains of the light dimming voices pierce through my vulnerability. Eventually, I befriend myself and return to the stone with more patience and a degree of self-compassion. Each time I am creatively generous with myself, I gain a sense of my wholeness and overflow with appreciation for the earth. Clay and stone are earth. I too am of the earth and the dust of faraway stars. Together we co-create and grow in love.

Clay As Teacher

Clay is also a teacher for me. The earth speaks to me when I hold it in my hands. Today I asked Squidge, "So is it like I am saying Hello to clay when I make the first gesture by putting my hands around a mound of clay?"

She shook her head and said, "No, Rosie. Think of it as the wind blowing a leaf or the ocean meeting the shore. It is always a reciprocal process."

A few hours later, I forgot the basic principles of co-creating. I pushed with my will to force the clay into a form that I held in my mind. The clay did not cooperate; I pushed harder. The clay resisted and weakened where I wanted it to strengthen. I persisted. Then it broke into several pieces. We both lost.

I felt bad and embarrassed and decided to take a walk around the pond. Another lesson about how when I allow my ego to override my best intentions, both harmony and creativity are sacrificed. I am learning that feminine creativity is about allowing rather than making things happen. I can almost hear Leonardo Da Vinci's voice echoing across centuries, "When the Spirit does not work with the body, there is no art."

Time and Creativity

Today Squidge invited me to take my time when creating art. In my whole life, I do not believe anyone ever invited me to take my time. Growing up, I was expected to arrive ahead of time. Hurry up became a life style. I graduated from college in three years with honors as a single Mom with a young son. I prided myself on my ability to push against time and declared myself a winner!

Squidge sensed I was battling with time and confronted me gently saying, "If being with clay is feeling like work or you are growing impatient, take a break. Do something that brings you pleasure. Never will yourself to create."

To imagine time as an ally—not an enemy is a radical act for me. Checking in with my body to determine what I need shifts everything. I grabbed my backpack and hiked. Along the way I wondered how my life might have been different if I had taken my time. Then I treated myself to a leisurely swim. Floating felt self indulgent and I reminded myself that I am a student of creative generosity and vowed to be compassionate with myself even when I do not relax perfectly!

When I emerged from the pond, I took time to notice the shapes and textures of the flowers, ferns and grasses that surrounded me. Then I noticed how the shadow of my right hand covered the paper as I wrote, the intricate patterns of a large green fern, the slenderness of an azure dragonfly that landed on the edge of my page, and the whirligig shape of the white clovers.

Then I surrendered to an afternoon nap. My senses felt like they were overloaded. I felt like I was yeasting: bubbling and fermenting—specific forms undifferentiated yet resting as potential.

My creative process asks of me: patience, curiosity, perseverance and humor. It demands I leave my mind, my lists, my questions and my tendency to overachieve and analyze outside of my studio.

Writing, too, is a creative act. I journal every day and I am amazed annually when I review my year's journal and discover how often creativity stalked me. When I intentionally collaborate with my guides and teachers, new dimensions of creativity emerge and I feel in awe. I often giggle as I imagine we each have "genius genes" and creativity is part of our DNA.

Creativity and Solitude

Earlier today my new neighbors approached me as I sat outside filing a 50-pound peach alabaster stone. The children seemed fascinated that I could make a shape out of stone.

Then the youngest girl asked, "What are you making?"

I said, "I don't know yet. The stone has not told me what it wishes to become yet."

She insisted that I tell her what the stone would turn into. I repeated that I did not know. Then I tried to explain that I was not in charge. My job was to listen, trust and then file. Her mother glanced at me and then said that maybe her daughter could come back and sculpt with me when she changed her clothes.

"Yes," said Elisabeth, I am creative and I can sit still and not fuss like my sister."

I hesitated for a few seconds, recalling when I would have gone along with entertaining Elisabeth. For decades I excelled at doing open house with my time and energy.

However, as I invest more deeply in my creativity, I take my time and energy more seriously. I took a long breath and then I said, "I would like to invite you to join me. However, I need to listen to the stone. I don't know how to do that when I have company. I'm sorry, maybe we could visit when I am not sculpting."

She looked disappointed and said, "I get it."

Hours later when I took a tea break, I tripped over a book by Oriah Mountain Dreamer, author of *What We Ache For: Creativity and the Unfolding of the Soul,* that fell open to a page with this quotation: "And we cannot let go, cannot surrender to the creative process itself unless we find some stillness and cultivate enough comfort with that stillness to allow ourselves to stay with the creativity of a fertile abiding emptiness that finds us." Oh, yes, I agree.

Surprises and discoveries arrive out of the blue when I release control—especially my need to know the outcome. Being open to all the possibilities connects me to my soul and frequent God gasps. When I am sculpting stone, I am present with an open heart and an open mind. Nothing more exists for me at that moment. I am aware that not only do I risk discovery—I also risk failure.

⊕ Things To Do

- Record places and times of beauty in your journal.
- Recall three things that enchant you with their beauty.
- Visualize a seesaw with creativity as the fulcrum. On one side of the board write the word Fear. On the opposite side write the word Excitement. Be aware of where the fulcrum is balanced and what you can do about that.

○ Stretching Questions

What aggravates, irritates and eats your creative energy?
In what ways do you express and honor your creativity?
As a creator, whom do you choose to be?
In what ways do you treat yourself with creative generosity?
What action are you willing to take right now to claim more of your creative potential?

♡ Quotations To Take to Heart

"I am a performing artist. I perform adoration."
>Mary Oliver

"Beauty is the explosion of energy perfectly contained."
>Richard Holmes

"With creative thoughts come health, wellness of the body, and wellness of the mind. Pepper Lewis

"The only kind of beauty that does not fade and that does not cause suffering is a compassionate and liberated heart." Buddha

"To the imagination the sacred is self evident." Nietzsche

"At the deepest level, creativity is holiness."
>John O'Donahue.

Part Three

Soul Story

Chapter Nine

Listen to Your Life for Your Soul Story

"If we respect the inner life, we find that it is also possible to reverse the whole relationship between inner and outer, beneath and above, and make the inner life come first, as a garden that is tended for its own sake...it opens for us the magic in everyday life."

John Tarrant

AS we commit to consciously living our evolving soul story, we enjoy a more fluid relationship to life. We become more comfortable living from a place of unknowing rather than foreclosing on options because we are motivated by fear. Sensing the mystery opens us up to expanded possibilities and new levels of freedom and meaning.

I offer the story of my last vision quest as an example of crossing a threshold.

My bones knew it was time to take another vision quest. The last time I survived a three-day vision quest was in 1995 when I was fifty-one years old. Although I am older, I am also stronger because of my twice a week Pilates classes. I wanted to dive deeper into my soul story. In anticipation of my vision quest, I wrote down a quotation from Rania Maria Rilke in case I needed reminding:

"Have patience with everything that remains unsolved in your heart and try to love the questions themselves, as if they were locked rooms and like books written in a foreign language. Don't search for answers, which could not be given to you now, because you would not be able to live them. And the point is to live everything. Live your questions now. Perhaps then, someday far in the future, you will gradually, without even noticing it, live your way into the answers."

Exposing myself to the elements of the Sangre De Christos Mountains, outside of Taos, New Mexico, for four days and three nights felt like another soul call, or jumping off place, despite some fear that my ego clobbered me with. I fasted for three days prior to the climb up the mountain and prayed to surrender and allow Spirit to lead.

The trek up the mountain on a horse was easier than I had anticipated and I was grateful that he was sure footed. No props—only a blanket and an extra large thermos filled with water and the earth, sky and me. Like before, I arranged my prayer ties in a large circle and sat in the center. About twilight, I opened my eyes after praying out loud for about three hours. About ten feet in front of me stood a large brown mother bear and her two cubs! For a few seconds I thought I might be hallucinating because of the three day fast I completed before the climb up the mountain and the unfamiliar high altitude. Then I saw the breath of the bear and panicked. My long-term memory kicked in and I remembered in rapid motion every single Davy Crockett movie I had viewed as a kid, especially the one where Fess Parker stared down the bear.

My heartbeat quickened. My arms and legs felt heavy. I knew I could not out run the bear. I also knew a mother bear is a dangerous animal when she has cubs. My mind accelerated to match my rapid heartbeat and breath. I imagined friends saying to one another, "It figures. Rosie was always a little weird. But she died pursuing her vision and that figures, too. She is probably happy."

I continued to stare at the bear afraid of what could happen. I knew I was a potential feast for this bear and heard myself saying, "Not again." The strength of my voice surprised me. Where had that verbal memory come from I wondered since I had no conscious memories of being devoured by an animal. Then I convinced myself that my only choice was to decide how I would die. I opened my heart and chose to remember times of beauty, gratitude and peace in preparation for my dying time.

All this time, I never took my eyes from the bear. I watched as she whacked one of her cubs with her big paw and ambled off into the woods. My body shook uncontrollably. When I was able, I stood up and walked to the spot where the bears had stood—still trying to prove to myself that this encounter had actually happened in real time rather than in my imagination or an alternate reality.

When I returned to the circle and my blanket and water, my mind swirled with questions. What did the bear mean? What was I supposed to learn? Why now? Why me? Why is this happening for me? I respected that the purpose of a vision quest is to wrap your heart around what the future is asking of you. I also believe that we attract circumstances and people into our lives in order to grow and move from personal story to soul story. Furthermore, I know that coincidences are opportunities to dive deeper into meaning making. I wondered if facing my own death was one of my lessons.

The next day I awoke early in the cold air. I had no memory of dreams. Throughout the day I prayed quietly and then sang prayers to the sky, the earth and the tall aspen trees. I walked in the small circle to preserve my strength and drank the cool water from my thermos. About twilight, I remembered the bear's visit from the night before. Then I blinked, looked up to find the family standing just where I'd seen them before. I laughed, surprised that curiosity had replaced my initial fear. Then I adjusted my eyes to look more closely at the mother bear.

This time I beheld the big furry creature with the eyes of a sculptor, noticing her shape and colors and the contours and texture of her massive body. Suddenly my thinking stopped as I merged with the bear's energy, just like I merge with a person when doing a soul reading. All I remember feeling was love. My heart opened to "bearness" and I knew in my bones that I would risk my life to protect this animal.

I returned to my physical body in time to see the mother bear lumbering into the woods, followed by her two playful cubs. I tried to remember if there had been any communication between us and then let go of that idea. My heart was filled with reverence and love. I had no energy to track meanings. Then I cried, remembering that I had not said Goodbye and Thank you to my new friend.

When I managed to stand up, I again walked slowly over to the same area where the bears had appeared and disappeared. I felt an overwhelming grief and love for the bear and myself. I missed her and the thought that I would never see her again felt unbearable. (Please excuse the pun.)

When I returned to the small, enclosed circle to reflect on my experience, my ego interfered and tried to convince me that I must be a slow learner because the bear had returned a second time and I was still clueless. I dismissed the light dimming accusation.

Then I remembered that I had been sculpting a small six-inch bear out of alabaster before I left on my trip. This was a perfect example of quantum thinking, which says that there is no such thing as cause and effect and that everything exists simultaneously. However, this "coincidence" left me feeling dizzy.

I slept a few times during the day. Dreams arrived. In one dream I reminded people how to live and die consciously. In another I had returned to teaching and I understood that teaching was another soul call. I made a commitment to teach people how to remember all of whom they were.

The next day as I gathered the prayer flags, I felt a huge shift in my consciousness and I intuited my cry for vision had been heard. While I folded my blanket, I caught sight of the Mommy bear. It was almost noon—not the usual time for bears to prowl for food. Once again my heart expanded and I was aware this would be an okay place and time to die. I watched as the bear and her two cubs walked in a straight line in front of me without stopping. I screamed, "Thank you for being a teacher and I accept."

Before I broke camp I made the following vows:

I vow to return to being a spiritual teacher.
I vow to remind others to awaken to their mystical longings and wisdom.
I vow to be more present to collaborate with God.
I vow to remind people how to die consciously.

It is not too late to make choices and changes that align you with your larger story. You do not have to fly to New Mexico and do a vision quest to align more deeply with your soul story. Direct experience is expansive and gains the attention of your heart. Any time you follow your inner calling, you move into the energetic field of Loving, Being and Becoming.

Consider the following soul principles as a compass as you live even more deeply into your unique soul story.

- Your soul is that part of you that is universal and unique at the same time.

- Your soul is the fullest expression of your Spirit—your connection with eternity.
- You soul is the dimension of unlimited possibilities.
- Your soul resonates with unconditional love, thinking and compassion.
- Your soul is the place of mystery, depth and delight.
- Your soul is the agent of transformation.
- Your soul is that part of you that touches and is touched by the world.
- Your soul is the place of conscious co-creation.
- Your soul resonates with beauty, greater expression and greater expansion.

Each time we expand our consciousness by moving beyond limiting patterns, our ego shrinks. You will know when you have transformed a limiting belief because your perspective and your expression will expand.

As you commit more deeply to living your soul story, be aware that your ego voice will try to imitate your soul voice. Remember that ego lacks a visionary perspective and it values the status quo. To discern between your different voices, remember to ask yourself: Does this information resonate with love?

If you desire more clarity, take a few conscious breaths and imagine that you have already acted on your inner guidance. Track how you imagine yourself feeling. Then shake your body free of that experience. Then return to your breath and imagine that you did **not** act upon your inner guidance. Track how you imagine feeling. Then shake your body free of that information. Remember your body is the delivery system for your soul.

Recently a woman asked to speak to me after a presentation I gave at the Maine Holistic Center in Bangor, Maine. She said she was confused about a persistent idea that she could not get out of her mind and she wanted to be certain the message was from her soul—not her ego. The recurring message told her it was time to expand her healing practice to include gallery readings. She told me that she was very comfortable seeing people privately in her office at home but felt apprehensive about being in front of a group of people. I suggested she move into her future and imagine giving healing messages and hands on healing to a group of people. She gasped and said, "I feel excited and lit up and I know this is a jumping off place for me."

"Where do you know that in your body?" I asked.

She pointed to her heart. We hugged and I reminded her to always remember that our body is our pendulum for truth.

Soul's Invitation

You soul will always invite you deeper into yourself as it challenges your personality's beliefs about self, others and the world. Opening up to experience other possibilities and new levels of freedom, creativity, prosperity and well-being connects us with our spacious, multi-dimensional selves. Soul also reassures us that nothing in our past limits our future. The essential question soul asks is: Who would you have to become to sustain a bigger life in order to bring deeper meaning to your experience? Seldom is the complete journey outlined in advance. Entering the mystery of soul story requires that you take the first step without knowing in advance what more will be asked of you. It is a dance between what is revealed and what is concealed. Full faith is required because a soul call may bring your entire life into question. Think of a soul call as an invitation that will not go away.

Your soul story is a combination of trusting and vulnerability, contentment and surrender, mastery and mystery. Our soul story calls us toward what is most unique within us. Being authentic means acting on the deepest truth each moment of our lives. The process of becoming our authentic self is one of the most impactful contributions we can make in our own families as well as the world. Authenticity and integrity are foundations for soul story. Think about authentic power as the human experience without the limitations of fear, self-doubt and self-hatred. Power includes the ability to see our selves clearly, to trust our instincts, and manifest our potential. Stepping into and owning your power is also acknowledging what triggers you into reactive behaviors. In other words, authentic power is the alignment of your personality with your soul.

We each have a unique frequency. What we experience depends on the frequency of our consciousness. Once you take the first step toward embracing your unique soul story, your perspective expands. You become the recipient of intuition, inspiration, dreams and synchronistic events. Gradually, you realize that you are in a reciprocal relationship with your guides, God and your own future.

Here is a short list of jumping off places that placed me squarely in my unfolding soul story:

- An unwanted emergency hysterectomy when I was 32 years old.
- The sudden death of my 14-year-old son, Mike, when I was 33 years old.
- A two-week excursion to Egypt when I was 40 years old.
- A name change to Deer Heart when I was 44 years old.
- A move from Maine, my home for four decades, to Taos, New Mexico where I knew nobody when I was 47 years old.
- An invitation to be a resident grandmother for my two young grandchildren when I turned 60 years old.
- A month's residential artist retreat when I was 67 years old.
- A four-month commitment to ecstatic prayer when I was 69 years old.
- A geographical move to Virginia Beach, Virginia when I was 69 years old.

Soul evolves. When we say yes to our soul's calls, we will finally know who we are beyond all illusions, projections, limiting beliefs and our small ego selves. Ending pretense and letting go of illusions allows for more soul presence. When we begin to taste who we can be without limitations, we become deeply aware that if we step into our larger soul story, we will have a powerful impact on our life, as well as the lives of others.

Sometimes a place or an event will open your heart to the presence of your unfolding soul story. That's what happened to me when I attended my first Pow Wow in Taos, New Mexico. Before the dancing and drumming began, the announcer asked for everyone's reverence—not attention. The boisterous crowd grew silent. My heart opened and I recognized that I was about to participate in a sacred ritual. Later I wrote in my journal that I appreciated that reverence feels like a soul memory. Then I remembered one of my favorite quotations from John O'Donahue, "All holiness is about learning to hear the voice of your own story."

Here are some ways to upgrade your frequency and move you into your soul story:

- Appreciate that you are the first choice of your soul.
- Choose curiosity over fear of the unknown.
- Reflect on the joy potential before making a decision.
- Adopt gratitude, generosity and grace as companions.
- Bless someone with your energy every day.
- Believe all is possible now.
- Says Yes to awakening your inner resources and manifesting your full potential.
- Embody your unique soul qualities.
- Respect silence and solitude as much as conversation and community.
- Befriend and celebrate with others who embrace their radiance.

~I invite you to breathe into your high heart and create an intention to remember your unique soul calls, the transformational jumping off places in your life. Then make a list. You also may wish to consider the invitations to jumping off places that you have resisted.

Here are some deepening questions to consider as you wrap your heart around each soul call as a jumping off place:

- What was the cost of answering the call of soul?
- What was gained?
- What was sacrificed?
- Who got left behind?
- Who showed up or accompanied you?
- What does your soul story require you to give to the world as opposed to what you want to give?

Answering your unique soul's call requires you to go beyond what you imagined and envisioned possible and give yourself permission to be brilliant, outrageously loving, creatively self expressive and in touch with your healing capacities and all other dimensions of your soul's story. Wholeness—not perfection is both the quest and the delight. My friend Barbara Cook, signs her emails: "Be Great" and I respond "And be grateful."

Not everyone answers the call. Here are some of the attitudes and beliefs that block the soul call:

- Rigid Thinking
- Inertia
- Comparison
- Self Judgment
- Self Abandonment

Soul Purpose as Truth in Your Life Story

> *I slept and dreamed that life was joy.*
> *I awoke and saw that life was service.*
> *I acted and behold, service was joy."*
> Rabindranath Tagore Bengali, poet and philosopher

I have enjoyed doing thousands of soul readings over the last thirty-five years. Each time I channel, I am amazed how individual each soul purpose is. We are all geniuses in terms of the inner architecture of our soul agreements.

Think about soul purpose as a question that will not go away.

Trust that your soul purpose will evolve as your consciousness expands. Vocation, or soul purpose, is a calling for your unique soul expression. Parker Palmer, author of *A Hidden Wholeness: The Journey Toward An Undivided Life* writes**,** "Vocation does not come from a voice 'out there' calling me to be something I am not. It comes from a voice 'in here' calling me to be the person I was born to be, to fulfill the original selfhood given me at birth by God."

My experience is that each time I said "Yes" to an aspect of my soul purpose, I merged with an aspect of my future self. There are no guarantees about what will happen when we act upon a soul call. The choice to live from our soul seldom conforms to our previous personal history and takes us to the edges of what we imagined or believed we were capable of becoming or being. I have returned to the challenge my advisor gave me during graduate school many times: "The less you risk, the more you lose when you win." I puzzled over his words for months before I began to live into them. As I gradually grew beyond my personal story, I used his words like a mantra to remind myself that my future depended on my ability to risk. My ego, or rational mind, rebelled and spewed out many of my cherished limiting beliefs.

Gregg Levoy, author of *Calling,* wrote that "Saying 'Yes' to the call tends to place you on a path that half of yourself thinks doesn't make a lot of sense, but the other half knows your life won't make sense without. The later half pushes out from within like a centrifugal force, keeps driving us toward authenticity, against the tyranny of fear and inertia and occasionally reason, against terrific odds and against knowing in our hearts that signals the hour." In the absence of knowing your soul's purpose, you risk being caught in the pressures of time, circumstances, and situations.

These questions will help you connect with the shape of your soul story:

- In what ways do you relate to your life as sacred?
- In what ways do you source your soul story?
- Who are the main characters in your soul story?
- What are the predominant themes in your soul story?

A question I often hear in my soul reading sessions is: How could I create a new kind of livelihood that is in alignment with my soul purpose? Consider these examples of switching livelihoods from what others expected of us to what our souls need us to embody.

Gene was a successful chief financial officer. He described himself as "going through the motions" and he dreaded Mondays. His soul purpose was connected to healing. When I raised the possibility that he might consider how he could bring healing energies to his current work place, he brightened up.

Morris was a young man whose soul purpose was connected to creating music. He entered engineering school to please his parents and flunked out although his professors referred to him as a "brilliant" student. When I suggested he take a year off and travel to other countries and listen to indigenous music, he cried.

Karen, an ordained minister, described her heart as needing life support. Her soul purpose was connected to the exploration and integration of her sexuality. Although she was scared her parishioners might find out, she signed up for a survey course on Tantric Sexuality. Later she left the ministry to teach sacred sexuality.

Our soul's gift is to make us more whole—not perfect. If you find yourself wondering if your profession is in alignment with your soul purpose, first let your mind know that you are open to entertaining possibilities. Then activate your will. Surrendering personal will, which is attached to appearance and outcome, and aligning with divine will connect you with your intuition.

Soul Qualities

Soul qualities are resources and values we brought into this lifetime. Our power and our healing are connected to our soul qualities when we embody them. My grandson, Noah, refers to our soul qualities as our super powers. I think about soul qualities as mega magnets that connect us to our soul purpose as long as we embody them. In other words, we have to take action—not just think or write about them.

Soul qualities include optimism, courage, trust, focus, clarity, and creativity. Keep in mind that each soul quality also contains its shadow polarity. For example, the shadow or ego aspect of optimism is pessimism. The ego aspect of trust is distrust. Two of my soul qualities are compassion and joy. I know when judgment and boredom come up that I am danger of being pulled into my personal story.

If you wish to gain further insight on your unique soul qualities I recommend asking four people who know you the most deeply what they consider unique about you. Then reflect on which traits may be soul qualities and make a choice to act on them.

Soul Affiliations

Soul affiliations add another pathway for guidance. Remember energy is information and information comes in many forms and from many dimensions. Some people consider soul affiliations as their allies.

Eileen Caddy, author of *Opening Doors Within* and co-founder of Scotland's, international community known as Findhorn, had a powerful soul affiliation with the Nature realm, as does her friend David Spangler, author of *The Laws of Manifestation*. The gardens at Findhorn are legendary for gorgeous vegetables and plants that flourish in less than ideal soil and have attracted people from all over the world.

Malia, my grand daughter has a strong connection to the Fairy realm. When she was seven years old she built large fairy villages, which included schools, hospitals, churches, parks and motels in our backyard.

Buckminster Fuller, author of *Operating Manual for Spaceship Earth* enjoyed a connection with light geometry and used it to inspire many of his geodesic designs.

Sometimes friends are more attuned to our soul affiliations than we are. For example, my friends have given me plants, crystals, and angels for my birthday forever. When I was involved in an intimate relationship, one day my partner shouted in frustration "What is it you want from our relationship?"

Without thinking, I said honestly, "Flowers and space."

We both laughed because we both recognized those were two of my soul affiliations.

Determining your soul qualities is easy. Align with your open mind and your open heart to engage your inner witness. Take a breath and let go of any preferences or attachments to a particular affiliation. Remember you may enjoy more than one soul affiliation.

Soul Affiliations include but are not limited to:

Nature realm: plants
Mineral: inner earth realm crystal, caves, volcanoes
Elementals: fire, water, air and earth
Fairy Realm
Angelic Realm
Space Realm: interdimensionals, UFOs, and Stellans
Light Geometry

Beginning with the Nature realm and going down the list, ask:

- Do I have a soul agreement to bridge my consciousness with yours?
- If you receive a yes response, inquire about the precise nature of your agreement.
- Then ask, what do you need from me?
- Next ask, how do you wish to serve me?

Soul Families

Soul families are united by their soul intentions and their previous soul history. Soul family members, like chosen evolutionary buddies, appear in our life to remind us of our soul purpose and our soul agreements. They challenge and support us to take responsibility for fulfilling our soul purpose and soul agreements, which I call our evolutionary obligations. They also encourage us to live more deeply from our hearts. Each member of our soul family is an agent of evolution with a specific assignment to remind us of anything that we have forgotten or are blinded to in relationship to our healing, karma, service and claiming the sovereignty of our authentic self.

Often upon first meeting a member of your soul family, you may be surprised that you do not need to catch up on the personal details of your lifetimes because a soul connection creates the context for moving ahead. You may feel a luscious sense of compatibility and safety with members of your soul family because you are aware of the fabric of each other's being. That happens when we have traveled together throughout time.

Recently, I was the guest at a party given by a new friend. Her home was on the ocean and the tide was coming in as we gathered for conversation and cocktails. I looked across the room and spotted a woman who looked familiar although I intuited that we had not yet met this lifetime

When I introduced myself, we both smiled. I wanted to say, "Sweet to be together again," but I let go of my impulse. Since I read energy, I knew she felt a strong connection to me, too and we reached out and hugged and then began speaking to each other from our souls.

Absent, too, is the need to protect your heart. The love, which grounds the "new" friendship, bridges lifetimes. The abiding intimacy is intense and strangely comfortable. It can also be seductive, especially if you lack the discernment to ask the question: "Is this person a member of my soul family or is he/she a soul mate, or both? However, always consider that your new beloved may be a member of your soul family and not a soul mate or "eternity partner" before you make a binding statement.

If you do not discern between soul family or soul mate, you risk setting yourself up by believing that you belong together and then you might leap to expectations for a long term committed relationship. Soul relationships can get messy when one or the other or both fantasize that "You are THE ONE."

Remember to lead with your Big Mind. Unconditional thinking is essential. Let the future be simple.

Although the nature of the soul agreement is to challenge, when necessary, as well as to provide a safe harbor for one another, the relationship may be temporary. Let it be simple and loving and honoring of the soul agreement. Perhaps you have a mutual agreement to open your hearts even more. Or maybe you have an agreement to heal some emotional or sexual wounds. Perhaps it is an agreement to remember a past lifetime that impacts and limits your freedom this lifetime.

Since we have all existed many times, it makes sense that we have enjoyed many partners. I do not believe that we have only one soul mate. I also do not believe that our soul mates are always of the opposite sex. Soul relationships have different purposes. Some relationships are teacher-student relationships, platonic relationships, romantic relationships or soul mate relationships (heart-mind-body-soul). Knowing the nature of the agreement makes it easier to fulfill our spiritual contracts.

To discern the nature of your relationship, breathe into your heart and invite your witness to provide clarity as you respond to these questions:

- Write their name.
- Without a preference, ask does this person share a destiny thread with me?
- What is the nature of our soul contract?

When I met Steve a few months ago, I intuited he was both a new friend and an eternal friend. Since the sudden death of my son Mike decades ago, I no longer hold back when I feel a strong connection to someone. Since I am familiar with soul family reunions, I expressed my love and appreciation out loud to him. We both knew that our friendship had the potential to grow deeper. However, he misunderstood my initial enthusiasm and authentic expression assuming I was interested in a committed relationship. He was not. We were honest with one another and agreed to continue to grow, support and interact as soul friends. Before parting we both agreed that our connection was deep, rare and juicy.

Calling In Evolutionary Buddies

The role of evolutionary buddies is to support you to live your life at high beam. Sometimes they use tough love. Sometimes they use silence. Think of them as your spiritual mirrors who reflect your sacred stories. When friends and family become scared, confused, or threatened by who you are becoming and want to "freeze" you into your past roles, your evolutionary buddies will challenge you to grow into your future self because they have no investment in who you used to be. Their investment is in who you are becoming. Count on your evolutionary buddy to confront you with questions like:

- What is your responsibility in this?
- In what ways are you repeating a limiting pattern?
- What is it you want me to most appreciate about you and this situation?
- What's the most evolutionary response you can make?
- What is the most compassionate response you can offer?
- How is this perfect?

The following Druid Vow of Friendship is an invitation to live from your soul story.
I bring an unprotected heart to our meeting place.
I hold no cherished outcome.
I will not negotiate by withholding.
I am not subject to disappointment.

I know from direct experience that the more I live into my evolving soul story, the fewer people accompany me on my journey. I used to think that community meant a large number of people. Now I am content interacting and interbeing with a few people who receive me from the inside out.

Self-validation becomes a skill for high beam living and loving. No longer does it serve us to look outside ourselves for recognition and acceptance. Self-care, self-acceptance, self-love and self-appreciation are friends of the soul.

It took me decades to figure out that I need to focus on my own journey and retire from co-starring in the countless invitations to participate in the drama of others. I remember the day I discovered that I had the choice to be happy even if people I loved were in the midst of their painful personal story. Malia learned that happiness is a choice when she was eleven and wisely reminds her friends that they are in charge of how they respond to life.

People sometimes describe me as courageous. I think of myself as a journeyer and I know deep in my heart that my journey is one of love. Keeping my heart open is a choice. Sometimes it breaks. Eventually it heals. I am bold enough and old enough now to believe that we are all on a journey to love. It does not matter what we love—another person, family, country, music, or even a bear.

The essence of our soul story is grounded in love. That is one of the reasons I enjoy beginning each day by following the simple affirmation that Ram Dass lives: I am love loving.

⊕ Things To Do

To listen to a Soul Affiliation Meditation, please visit my website at: www.heart-soul-healing.com

✺ Stretching Questions

What is your biggest yearning?
How do you know when you are being faithful to your soul story?
What is your spiritual potential?
What is your Presence in the world based on?
In what ways do you honor your inner life?

♡ Quotations To Take to Heart

"Look for the Goodness in every event, relationship and even catastrophe. That perspective will move you into a spiritual perspective."
Big Angel

"For our own good, each of us needs to know what our mission is, because the details of how we live our lives accumulate to create health or illness." Caroline Myss

"The soul needs an intense, full bodied spiritual life as much as and in the same way that the body needs food." Thomas Moore

"Each person that wakes up to their purpose in the larger scheme of things vibrates with an intensity that is inspirational to others. These actions reverberate throughout the web, through our relations, into the collective. We awaken ourselves by relating more deeply to what's around us." Anodea Judith

"The place where you are right now, God circled on the map for you." Hafiz

"Our task is to say a holy Yes to the real things in life."
Natalie Goldberg

"Jump and you will find out how to unfold your wings as you fall."
Ray Bradbury

Chapter Ten

The Journey Toward God

PART of soul story is our journey toward God. What a surprise to recognize that while I was searching for God that God was also searching for me. Prayer, for me, is a rich inner experience that opens me up to a relationship with God and centers me in my soul story. It is a way to open my heart to new possibilities.

I am comfortable praying in private and I have a prayer pot filled with names of people who have asked for healing prayers that I pray over twice a day. As I look back over my life, I have always been shy about leading prayers publicly.

However, when I receive the same invitation more than two times in a relatively short period of time, I listen inwardly and outwardly. I have learned that synchronistic events are meant to grab our attention and move us in the direction of merging with our future selves.

I took notice when for the sixth time in five weeks I was asked to pray publicly. The first time came as no surprise since I had volunteered to facilitate a friend's celebration of life. The second time did not feel out of the blue either because I agreed to lead prayers for another Pilate's student who was in the hospital. A day later I said yes to lead a group prayer in my Bangor, Maine PEO group for sisters who were in need of healing. Although people complimented me about my prayers, I knew that I held back and did not allow the Divine to have its way with me. That made me dissatisfied with myself and also curious.

Tracking my own consciousness can be tricky. Encountering and integrating my personal shadow is on-going work. That is one of the primary reasons that I meet with my spiritual advisor, Megan Don, monthly. She begins each session with a prayer. Then I offer up whatever is in my heart.

I began a recent session by describing how stuck I felt trying to figure out how to end this book and said I had a strong intuition that I had missed a crucial step in bridging personal story and soul story. Then I took a breath and reviewed my story of agreeing to pray publicly and applying brakes, admitting that I felt like I was in the throes of my personal story. I added that my resistance to full faith praying publicly felt like a hard basketball in my stomach. When I finished, Megan paused and then asked me if I shut down my energy field when I meditated, channeled or prayed privately.

"Of course not," I replied. "What would be the point?"

Then she asked me if I was aware of what held me back from making a strong connection to the full power of prayer.

Without thinking, I responded "Passion and power and standing out." How instantly I knew surprised me, as did the strength of my words. I felt a bit dizzy, and realized I'd stopped breathing. Then I took a gentle breath and comforted myself by reminding myself that soul works that way—it surprises and leaves me feeling a bit undone and out of control.

Megan asked if I had considered that a past lifetime might be bleeding through my consciousness. When she asked that pivotal question, Goddess bumps erupted all over my skin. My grandmother called the bumps "goose bumps" and I renamed them "Goddess bumps." My heart beat faster, my cheeks felt hot, and I had an inner sense of rightness—all green light signals for me.

Even though I still felt some fear, I asked my guides to open up the akashic records and requested to re-enter the original lifetime when this drama began. Swiftly I re-entered a lifetime in the early 1500's. I was a young woman, perhaps in my middle twenties and I had gained a reputation for speaking from trance, which was called ecstatic prayer. I was not conscious of the words I spoke. When I came out of trance I knew people who came to listen to me were deeply touched because of their tears and their words. Yet I had no memory of what I had channeled.

I listened to my words as if I were watching a movie. I heard, a familiar theme: "You have a direct link to God. You do not need priests, rabbis, or ministers to intercede on your behalf. God is your familiar—as in family." My words were filled with passion and truth. I was in rapture. My words connected people to their Divine nature and their Divine truth.

Still curious I asked to revisit another significant event in that lifetime and I witnessed my former self—holding my hands against my heart in pain. My heart felt like it had been pierced open and I feared I was having a heart attack. At that moment I could not discern if I were in present time or past time. Fortunately, I had the clarity to ask for guidance and heard the word "transverberation" which was foreign to me. Later when I had returned to ordinary consciousness, I looked the word up and it means," to be pierced by an arrow from the Divine."

Gradually recovering my breath, I asked to move to the end of this past lifetime. Moving ahead a few years, I was not surprised to witness myself being beheaded while I was in the midst of ecstatic prayer. I had been charged with heresy. No wonder I felt hesitant to pray publically! Trauma, whether past lifetime or present, creates a soul wound as well as an opportunity for healing.

Megan listened to my story without interrupting and then challenged me, "Rosie, what if one of your gifts this lifetime is passionate prayer?"

Goddess bumps erupted on my arms and then spread all over my body.

"Then I will welcome the opportunity to pray publicly," I said

"Good, be gentle. This is big."

Although I was relieved to have clarity about the origin of my fear, I felt impelled to reconnect to the devotional strand that I had remembered in order to reclaim my passion and move closer to my authentic self. On the spot I made a commitment to immerse myself in a daily practice of ecstatic prayer trusting that I would remember how as long as I followed through on my commitment. I had no idea or expectation about how long the commitment would last or who I might be when I emerged. I knew in my heart I'd come to another Jumping Off Place.

I am not a stranger to devotion this lifetime. For the past nine years I have focused my daily devotion on nurturing my two grandchildren. Malia and Noah spend the summer with their father so I had the space and freedom to fully immerse myself in ecstatic prayers. Everything was in its place—even me. I also let go of finishing the book you are now reading until I had healed this part of my own personal history.

When I am not captive to a traumatic past lifetime overlay, I understand that praying is another way of channeling Spirit. I teach that prayer has the power to uplift our vibrations and links us to our spiritual story. I also know that an essential theme of our soul's story is the journey toward God. I also appreciate, now that the past lifetime no longer overshadows this one, that prayer opens me up to a deeper relationship with the Divine. I cry when I imagine the power of Spirit coming through me as a gift this lifetime.

Prayers and The Big Smudge

When I searched my journals for examples of praying publically, I found this story.

It started as I sat beside the shallow creek which ran through my backyard in San Cristobal, New Mexico, sipping champagne and left over sandwiches from my book signing for *Healing Grief: A Mother's Story.*

A friend spotted smoke and asked, "Where is that smoke coming from?"

I couldn't tell for sure. It looked like near the one room post office at the bottom of the hill. I did know it should not be there. Without saying a word, we scrambled to our feet and raced to my car and headed down the winding dirt road.

The thick smell of smoke and the thudding sounds of trees falling to the ground alerted us to the whereabouts of the fire before we spotted the high flames. We pulled the car into a driveway already jammed with cars. Neighbors hollered for hoses, pails and shovels. I could not move nor take my eyes of the fiery rampage.

More cars screeched to a halt in the driveway. Local fire official's from nearby Hondo argued in Spanish with representatives from the National Forestry Service over who had authority to order people and tell them what to do.

I wanted to interrupt them and remind them that the trees belonged to all of us. I wanted to scream and tell them to do something, anything, except argue about jurisdiction. I resisted, reminding myself that I was an outsider in this small village. I was a single woman—one of four unmarried Anglos in a village of 108 Hispanic people. According to local legend, I was either a witch or a lesbian, maybe both.

Someone handed me a heavy shovel and ordered, "Cava." I clutched the tall shovel and joined others. I had no idea why we were digging a trench. Then I heard someone call my name. "Rosalie, come here. You no dig so good, but you pray strong. In an emergency, each must do what they do best."

I quickly handed my shovel to another volunteer and joined several men from Taos Pueblo. When I climbed into the old truck they told me they were headed up to the top of the mountain to pray for the "Big Smudge" to stop burning. Before we took off, a police car whizzed in front of us and blocked the one lane dirt road.

The sheriff announced a mandatory evacuation and gave me thirty minutes to gather my belongings.

"She goes with us" replied one of the elders with authority and pointed to me.

"There is only one road down this mountain and the same road goes up the mountain. You can be trapped up there if the winds turn and blow the fire back this way."

"We know," said one of the men.

"I can't let you go up the mountain, especially with her," bellowed the sheriff.

"I belong with them," I said in a loud voice. "I love this land. It feels like home to my soul."

Without more conversation, Tony turned the steering wheel to the right and swerved in front of the police car.

When we got to the top of the mountain, we found about 8 large logs blocking the entrance. Two National Guardsmen pointed to the hand painted sign which read, "For your safety, turn back and save your life."

Without a word, three of the men jumped off the flat bed, and tossed the logs aside. I watched in silence. One of the elders said over his shoulders to the two young guards, "This land needs our prayers. We have powerful pleas. We come in peace. The fire is not peaceful. We pray for this land that belongs to all of us." The two uniformed men backed away from the entrance, lowered their guns, and waved us on.

The men staked out their places. Then they began to pray loud, passionate pleas for the winds to die down. Eventually songs mixed in with prayers. It didn't matter that I did not pray to the bones of my ancestors. It did not matter that I only knew about 100 words in the Tewa language. I prayed silently at first. Then I closed my eyes. Then unrehearsed words came out of my mouth—strong, passionate prayers that commanded the big winds to show their kind power rather than their strong power.

We prayed in shifts—four people to a shift. A shift ended when at least two people were too exhausted to pray, sit or stand. When we were not praying, we slept. For five nights and five days, we kept a 24-hour prayer vigil. The women from Taos Pueblo who delivered fresh water and food to us told us 4,000 firefighters now lived in our small village and the fire had destroyed 7,500 acres of pristine forest. On the sixth day, the winds died down and the fire was contained.

My grief felt enormous. I wanted to mark the death of each tree and I knew that would take many lifetimes. I offered a prayer to the fallen trees, the dead animals, and the firefighters who helped us. Then I cried. My arms and hands pounded the earth—this earth that I loved. If only the earth could eat my grief. Then I listened. Missing were the howling winds and thuds of falling trees, the loud motors of the airplanes and the echoes that the bags of chemicals made when they thudded on the ground. Missing, too were the insistent prayers that punctuated the day and night. I moved my stiff legs and rested in a fetal position. Then I thanked the earth for cradling me.

Community prayer feels different to me than publicly praying alone. Yet I am glad I found this story in my journals because I know prayer has been stalking me for more than three decades.

The Power of Yes

I invite you to say a BIG Yes to life and ask God to do with you what he will, take you where he wants you to go and accept responsibility for making a change in the world. Then surrender your need to know how your future will evolve. If you try to force the future, the shape will resemble your personal story. Then empty yourself of all thoughts, concerns, and feelings so the winds of God can move through you.

My grandchildren are experts in reminding me of the interweaving strands of personal story and soul story. Malia, who is now twelve years old, questions me frequently about the details of my personal story. For example, she asks, "Grandmom, when you were my age were you a tomboy or a girlie-girl?" "What did you call your period?" and then looks shocked when I tell her we all called our monthly visitor, "our friend." Recently she asked, "What's the best way to get over a crush?" One of her most recent observations about boys her age was, "Grandmom, it is impossible for boys to know what girls they like since they can't even decide what they want for supper."

Noah, who is now nine, often makes observations that are connected to the threads of my ongoing soul story. For example, when he accompanied me to a doctor's appointment, he asked the chiropractor if he were friends with God. Later he told me "Never let anyone who does not know God as a friend touch your body, Grandmom."

In September I took Noah and Malia to visit St John's Episcopal Church in Bangor, Maine I wanted them to be comfortable finding me when their Sunday school program was over so I walked them down the wide center aisle to point out where I would be sitting. Noah stared at the tall vaulted ceiling, the full-length stained class windows, the large statues, and the ornate chandeliers. His mouth opened and his eyes got big.

He grabbed my hand, craned his neck to look up higher, and came to a halt when the organ music filled the church as the choir began to rehearse. As we approached the front of the church, he pulled my hand and said in a loud voice,

"Grandmom, I'll bet God likes coming to this beautiful church to worship us." People nearby chuckled.

I stooped to be closer to his ear and whispered, "Noah, that's not quite the way it goes. Remember, we come here to worship God."

He looked me in the eye and said, "Grandmom, don't you remember that God worships us when we worship him. It is all the same. We are like mirrors for each other."

I gulped, squeezed his hand, and said,

Thanks for reminding me, Noah."

"No problem, Grandmom, I told you I know that your brain is getting old and I will remind you of important stuff."

Here is a story about another one of my evolutionary buddies and a conversation we shared last summer.

Meredith Jordan and I were members of a women's healing circle that met four times a year back in the seventies and eighties to celebrate solstices, equinoxes and each other. When I moved to New Mexico, we lost touch with one another.

Years went by and each time we met in person, our long history called each of us to be present. We knew the heart openings and heart breaking personal stories of each other's lives as well as the soul calls and sacrifices we had each made to become more loyal to our soul story and our journeys toward God.

We met up in Ogunquit, Maine in the summer of 2013.

Over appetizers, Meredith asked, "How do you refer to God these days, Rosie?"

I gave myself a few moments to reflect because nobody had even asked me that question before.

"Mostly God, and sometimes The Divine," I answered.

She replied, "Remember all those years when we rebelled against the patriarchal names for God, because it excluded the feminine?"

"Yes, that is when we referred to God as "Mother—Father God and we designed a new language and liturgy honoring the feminine aspects of God."

"What changed for you?" Meredith asked with genuine interest.

"I wanted to enjoy a simple relationship with God and my life. Over time I have discovered that arguing about Divinity from a personal position creates gaps that deepen duality. I know from deep inside that God has no gender—only love and compassion."

"Amen," she said and we held hands and were silent.

Then I asked her to share her favorite God quotation. She couldn't decide so I treated her to my current favorite from Mother Theresa, "We are pencils in the hand of a writing God who is sending love letters to the world."

By the time supper arrived I shared with Meredith that I know from my direct experience that when I keep God present in my heart, God becomes a felt reality in my life. I enjoy how my friend Michael Lightweaver, author of *A Day of Grace,* summarizes esoteric principles and flavors them with his practical wisdom: "The pathway to God is in your heart."

Miracles

When I agreed to write *Awaken* in 2009 I knew I had said Yes to another soul call. I was excited and nervous to return to writing after a seven-year departure from writing as I devoted myself to being a residential grandmother to Malia and Noah. I wondered if my brain had atrophied or if I had anything meaningful to contribute. For sure, my self-confidence as a writer and spiritual teacher felt shaky. I had to remind myself that I had said yes to another soul call.

My old computer died just as I finished writing the first chapter of *Awaken.* Excited about writing again, lacking the money to buy another computer frustrated me. During the night I heard a reassuring voice say, "Trust. You will have a computer by this time tomorrow."

I knew I had not been dreaming. I distinctly heard the words. I got out of bed and walked to the kitchen to get a drink of water. On my way back to bed, I looked in the closet to see if someone was playing a trick on me. No matter how hard I tried, I could not make sense of the voice I had heard and I also could not dismiss it.

In the morning I went into the closet to get my clothes, and I stubbed my toe on something. I looked down to see what I had bumped up against and I spotted a pile of dollar bills—one hundred dollar bills. Twelve new one hundred dollar bills. Initially, I thought they might be counterfeit. Then I thought my daughter might have put them there. I was wrong on both counts.

Still not having an explanation, I drove to the computer store. When I handed the clerk the $1200, I asked him to check with his supervisor to make sure the money was real because I did not want to get anyone in trouble. Moments later I walked out of The Apple Store with a new computer and a one year tutorial agreement and just enough money left over to buy a cup of coffee.

I am convinced that miracles are natural occurrences even though I do not live in a culture that encourages people to be on the look out for miracles. However, if you dare to change your belief, miracles become normal.

While writing this book, I received another miracle. I had just finished re-writing a chapter when my friend Georgia joined me for our early morning meditation. She sat down in the rocking chair to enjoy a few more sips of her coffee and conversation before we meditated. The printer activated itself and spewed forth a page of writing that was not mine. We resumed our chat and the printer repeated the action. We both looked at two new pages that were neatly arranged in paragraphs and agreed that the concepts supported the themes in this book. While we were upstairs meditating in the loft, I thought I heard the faint hum of the printer again. Sure enough, when we came downstairs, another page set in the tray. I have sprinkled the writing throughout the chapters.

Journeying Toward Joy

When you commit to high beam living and loving, joy is contagious and others feel like they, too have permission to shine. A Tibetan master said "The whole of spiritual practice can be summarized in two words: "Be Spacious."

Last summer my soul friend, Leslie, and I enjoyed an extended two-day pajama party. One morning we enjoyed ourselves as we shopped for new costumes. Leslie is a fashion maven who has a knack for intuitively selecting the perfect outfits for us. After observing her for a couple of hours, I knew I was getting the hang of this "dress up" game. In our fourth store, I spotted a teal blue shirt and instinctively knew it would hang just right. I tried it on and posed in front of the full-length mirror. One of the sales ladies, looked over and said, "You look good."

Without thinking, I said, "No, I look great!" Women stopped looking for clothes, looked up, smiled, and then applauded. I curtsied and smiled back in delight.

Joy touched me one summer morning when I got up at five o'clock because I heard unfamiliar sounds outside by the pond. I spotted Noah lying on his stomach on the dock singing the Star Spangled Banner. I quietly joined him as he continued to sing. When he completed the second verse, he told me that he woke up with so much joy in his body that he had to sing to the fishes and the land.

"Why the Star Spangled Banner?" I asked.

"It's the only song that I knew that had two verses and I had a lot of joy to sing," he said seriously.

I am certain that Hafiz, who lived more than eight hundred years ago and Noah would have been good friends:

I am happy even before I have a reason.
I am full of light even before the sky
can greet the sun or the moon.

My new friend Barbara Cook, researcher and author of *The Science of Light Medicine* has committed her life to live as an example of God's love. She counts on God to be her provider, protector, and healer. Then she prays and listens for guidance, which often becomes revelation, and her life fills with

The Journey Toward God

love, joy, meaning, and abundance. Her favorite question to God is, "How can life be even better than this?" Because she lives her life with full faith, something even more glorious unfolds.

⊕ Things To Do

Listen to the channeling of Big Angel on my website at: www.heart-soul-healing.com.

Keep a miracle journal.

Begin to create joy moments each day so when you are in your dying time, you will remember moments of joy.

Create your own poem that begins with the first line of this poem.

God speaks to each of us as he makes us
Then walks with us silently out of the night.
These are the words that we dimly hear:
You, sent out beyond your recall,
Go to the limits of your longing.
Embody me.
Flare up like flame
And make big shadows I can move in.
Let everything happen to you: beauty and terror.
Just keep going. No feeling is final.
Don't let yourself lose me.
Nearby is the country they call life.
You will know it by its seriousness.
Give me your hand.

Ranier Maria Rilke

✺ Stretching Questions

- Do you dare to live your life with more presence and power?
- What would your life be like if everything worked out perfectly?
- Who would be with you?
- What would you be doing?
- Where would you be living?

What counts for being available to Spirit for you?
What is your faith history?
Where, when and with whom do you encounter God?
Where are the grace places in your life?
What legacy do you intend to create for future generations?

♡ Quotations to Open your Heart

"Miracles occur naturally as expressions of love."
Marianne Williamson

"As to me, I know of nothing but miracles."
Walt Whitman

"Humans have anxiety around pleasure. Think of pleasure as a sign of love of self. Allow yourself more pleasure in life in relationship to self and others. Pleasure has an energy that connects to soul as long as your chosen pleasure does not dim your light."
Big Angel

"Ask and the gift will come. Seek and you shall find. Knock and the door will be open to you." Luke 11:11

"When you possess light within, you see it externally."
Anais Nin

"The refusal of ecstasy is unknown in heaven."
Marianne Williamson

Chapter Eleven

The Cobwebbing Power of Destiny Threads

COBWEBS have fascinated me since I was a little girl. I remember staring at an unfinished cobweb and wishing I knew how to spin webs. Then I searched for spiders in hopes that I could watch how they did it. I never found a spider in the act of spinning a web. I found spiders and plenty of webs—sometimes sprinkled with early morning dew. But I never caught a spider in the act of spinning. Cobwebs introduced me to Mystery. My irresistible pull to the mystery of spiders did not end with childhood. I remember writing an article about hiring a spider as a consultant for one day when I was in my forties.

How spiders spin their webs from a filament inside their bodies still fascinates me. They work from the inside of the web to the outer edges. The threads of every single spider's web I have studied are always symmetrical. Although the threads are thin, they are strong and hold up during strong windstorms. Somehow in ways I have yet to understand cobwebs and soul stories are connected.

During a recent presentation I spoke about "destiny threads" and how surprised and grateful I am when I recognize another one of my destiny threads. I am beginning to appreciate that somehow when I am living and loving at full beam, I broadcast a wider frequency band and my energy field becomes an irresistible magnet that attracts people and events that resonate with what's called "wild cards" in quantum theory. Wild cards are always unpredictable and defy logic.

Tracking and appreciating our destiny threads is another way to support full beam living and loving. For example, well over thirty years ago when

I taught at the Creative Problem Solving Institute in Buffalo, New York, I ordered Alison Strickland, a stranger to me at the time, to come to my journal keeping session. Although I have earned a reputation for being an outrageous extrovert, I have never been that audacious.

Alison showed up at my class and we discovered that we both were English teachers, avid journal keepers, appreciators of wine and spiritual seekers. We have been friends for nearly four decades and we wrote *Harvesting Your Journals* together. She held me in her prayers even when I disappeared from myself. She's always supported my creativity and volunteered to take on the arduous task of editing *Awaken* and this book that you are reading.

Another example of a destiny thread that spans twenty-eight years is my connection with Dennis Kosciusko, a man who came to me for a soul reading in 1985. Fast-forward to 2013 and Dennis shows up at my presentation, Don't Retire—Inspire, in Bangor, Maine. He approached me after the talk, shook my hand and asked if my last name had always been Heart. I shook my head. Then he told me he still listened to the soul reading I did for him 28 years ago when my name was Rosie Byrer.

"I hope it was a good one," I laughed. He nodded and asked, "Do you still do workshops and retreats?" unaware that I had left my former life behind to become a fulltime resident grandmother.

"I have done a few residential workshops in southern Maine and I don't know of any places available in this area."

Then he told me he had built a retreat center in nearby Stetson, Maine and invited me to visit. I accepted on the spot! The story does not stop there. In the summer, fall and early winter of 2013, I lived at The Gathering Place with my four cats and almost finished writing this book.

Another important thread, which weaves into my present story, is connected with my son, Mike, Mother Mary and me.

My first encounter with Mary happened on the 15th anniversary of the death of my son, Mike on March 23, 1991. That was the year that he had been dead longer than he had been alive. I was not prepared for the deep sadness that I experienced when I realized that he belonged somewhere else more than to the life we had shared.

Two of my friends suggested we drive from New Mexico to Crestone, Colorado to meditate in a round church and then relax in a hot spring. I agreed. As soon as I entered the small round church and knelt down, Mother

Mary was present. That surprised me because I am not Catholic (this lifetime). Instantly, I was behind her eyes looking at myself with enormous compassion and love. I felt both realities simultaneously as the energy behind Mary's eyes and as myself, the individual she was beholding and loving. Overwhelmed by the intimacy and the enormity of the experience, I sobbed. When I could stand up, I felt different—like my center of gravity had been re-arranged and I would never be the same again. I remember telling my friends that I had received a healing and those words did not come close to the grace of heart that I felt. When we left the church, I noticed for the first time, a simple etched sign, which read "Mary's Sanctuary."

To follow the cobweb strand, move ahead twenty-two years. For four months—from August 9th to November 9th I devoted myself to the practice of ecstatic prayer in order to heal a traumatic past lifetime when I was beheaded for telling people they had direct access to God. By opening my heart and allowing myself to be receptive to my own soul's evolution, I once again consecrated my life to God. High Beam living and loving became as familiar as my breath.

I've captured my inner experiences during that time in these journal entries.

August 15, 2013

During my passionate prayer practice this morning, Mary, the Holy Mother, announced herself as if she had expected me. I bowed my head in reverence. Then she reached out and touched my face and hands with her light and invited me to join her by "uplifting."

I raised my head and beheld her as being miles high—as if she stretched to Eternity. No matter how high I stretched my physical neck, I could not see her face. Her long red robe created a column, which was made of light. I stepped into the light container.

With my inner ears I heard her say, "Uplift. It is your celestial nature, your essential nature. Uplift."

I began to lift off.

"More, more," she intoned.

When I reached her "level," with no memory of how that happened, we were together—not face-to-face—more light-to-light. She directed love into my heart.

I felt a bit afraid since the most recent piercing of my heart with light about 6 weeks ago was painful and I imagined I was having a heart attack.

After the painless, light transmission, which happened in an instant, the only words I remember saying were, "Your Grace, Your Grace."

She assured me I had received a transfusion of Light, which in our dimension is Love. (As I wrote the last word, after returning to my body, the following words appeared on my page)

"That is correct. You did."

That surprised me. Then I sobbed, "I have been waiting for this connection for— for— forever."

Inwardly, I heard her voice reply, *"Yes, lifetimes. Yes, allow the tears to overwhelm you and appreciate the rainbows you create with your tears. Remember it is only your physical body that feels overwhelmed by the spaciousness of light for you are skin and bones and organs and light."*

She gestured to me to follow her once again in the spiral of light. Out of my heart, not my eyes, I beheld Jesus kneeling in prayer like from an old picture I saw when I was a little girl. I watched and felt again overwhelmed with reverence and devotion. We did not interact.

Then I found myself in the light spiral, heading back to my physical body. The Holy Mother said to me, *"There will be more. You are ready. This was your introduction to indwelling prayer."*

When I felt grounded in my physical body once more, I noticed that my neck remained drawn upward. Then I noticed the early morning light coming through the window in back of me making my hands look like they radiated light. Then my third eye, in the middle of my forehead, began to pulsate. That felt painful so I lay down on the soft, green-carpeted floor. Then I noticed bubbly like sensations on the top of my head in my crown chakra.

A voice interrupted me as I tracked my sensations, *"With your permission…*

"Of course," I stammered out loud not needing to understand what I was consenting to because a deep sense of Rightness was more than enough.

Words spilled out of my mouth, "Praise to Thee, Praise to Thee" as energy rippled throughout my body. Then I felt chills. I lifted my arms to the side and upward, repeating, "Praise to Thee." In that moment praise felt like gratitude uplifted. My third eye pulsated even more rapidly and the pain disappeared. Then I smiled as I realized that the words "prays" and "praise" are homonyms!

I felt huge humility as I sent out praise and then became overwhelmed with light, adoration and silence. The energy field, which was me, filled with crimson red and it expanded as I deepened into my expression of praise. From far away I heard a voice channel, *"This is the royal red—the vibration of Divine Love. Welcome. Welcome."*

August 25th

In meditation this morning I beheld Mary again. This time she named herself The Lady of Light and I knew her as Mary. Unlike before, I did not merge with her. I remained in my own body. I felt enthralled as I watched her outstretched hands turn to light. Then her face, shoulders, mid-section and lower body radiated light. My shoulders dropped, unassisted by me and I jumped in surprise. Mary remained.

Because we occupied the same expanded, energetic field, I received the light that she radiated and I sent it out to the world. Receiving and giving, receiving and giving, the familiar gesture reminds me of one of my favorite Tai Chi movements. Tears streamed down my eyes. Later in the day I invited Mother Mary to channel her wisdom to me.

> Me: Thank you, Mother Mary, for being here.
> *Mother Mary: With pleasure. How may I serve you, Dear One of the Light?*
> Me: You just called me "Dear One of the Light. I am in tears and deeply touched. I cannot remember my question.
> *Mother Mary: Your surprise mystifies me. Of course, you are of the light. That is your lineage and your heritage, as it is for all of earth's people.*
> Me: (Sigh) I believe that, mostly. And my connection with you feels intimate as I experience it in my body. And that makes everything deeper and fuller and vaster and I am lost for the words.
> *Mother Mary: If the only word you had in your vocabulary was Love that would suffice.*
> Me: I want to relish your wisdom, without asking more questions.
> *Mother Mary: Bliss does that to human ones.*
> Me: Yes, I have felt the edges of bliss a few times in my life. It came as a surprise and then left as suddenly. When I meditate and pray daily I have a sense of bliss lingering even after I resume my daily life.
> *Mother Mary: You are making way for bliss and blessings in your heart.*

> *With practice you will walk through your day with bliss always within your reach.*

Me: Really? I am trying to imagine how that would be.

Mother Mary: *No need to try. I will give you a word to ground you into an expanded experience of yourself. Do I have your permission?*

Me: Yes, of course.

Mother Mary: *"Revelatory." Your experience of yourself, others and the world will be "revelatory."*

Me: (Big Breath.) That sounds very serious although when you first channeled the word to me, I immediately thought of "revelry" which I do enjoy. Then I understood you meant revelation—like deep truth.

Mother Mary: *Both are accurate. A mystical orientation need not be dull or serious, you know. You have read too many books. Yours is the path of joy and compassion.*

Me: And how do revelations fit in?

Mother Mary: *Perfectly My Dear One of the Light.*

Then she disappeared. And then I remembered I wanted to know what determined whether I blended, merged or fused. Suddenly, the distinctions no longer mattered.

August 27th

During the early moments of meditation this morning, I found myself studying hands again. Not Mary's, but the hands of my son, Mike that I remember from the last picture I took of him before he died. Imagine placing your two thumbs together forming a straight line. Then place your index fingers together and then the other three fingers, letting your two little fingers line up to match your thumbs. That is the form that he flashed in the Christmas picture. I have been intrigued with the shape of his hands in that picture since I saw it the first time. Intuitively, I understood that his hands held a mystery—a code that I could not decipher. The radiance of his face and the shape of his hands felt like they have been etched on my soul. I snapped that picture thirty-six years ago and it is as real to me as the tomato I enjoyed for breakfast this morning.

In meditation I saw his hands in the pyramid formation—not his body—just the hands. There is something about his hands. Without warning, I was behind his hands. Only this time I understood at an eternal level the meaning encoded in his cupped hands. His hands that I captured in the photograph announced his readiness, his agreement to die. The words "Source Code" whistled through my consciousness as I allowed the revelation to sink into my cells.

If my information was true, that meant that Mike had announced his readiness to die before he was electrocuted in the schoolyard three months later. Was his death, which I have always called "premature" or "sudden" before this moment, actually one of his destiny threads? What does that say about death or life and their connection?

I have never imagined dying as a co-creative act. I had never heard of flashing a Source Code. I always imagined that death was something that happened to us. We either resisted or allowed. But death as a co-creative act is a stunning concept.

Earlier today I made a decision to ask for more information about Source Code, dying and conscious co-creation. I felt nervous, like if I asked the questions, my consciousness will never again be familiar to me. Like I will be an orphan to all I have known and believed this lifetime. Yet my curiosity and an inner knowing that I was like a spider weaving its web gave me strength. Although I have no idea whom I am addressing, I open my heart and mind up to Beings of the light in all dimensions that are in alignment with this strand of destiny.

> *Voices: Thank you. Doubt not that you have been on this path for many lifetimes.*
>
> Me: From where I am sitting, I doubt almost nothing. I feel vulnerable and receptive at the same time.
>
> *Voices: Be at peace with your experience. Peace allows us to connect more deeply. There is no hurry. All will be revealed. We are a consortium— of sorts. Let's begin by reassuring you that your revelatory connections earlier are true. You bridged dimensions when you discovered yourself in back of him whom you knew in your dimension as Mike. When you merged with his hands and then separated, you experienced a deeper truth than you ever imagined possible. That is the way of the way. We pause now to honor your human response.*

Me: I feel overwhelmed and I know I have become bigger than myself during these three weeks of passionate prayer.

Voices: You have forever been vaster than your human Self, Dear One of the Light. You are also no stranger to bridging dimensions. Each time you remind someone of past lifetimes you are bridging dimensions. When you dream, you often bridge dimensions.

Me: I am comfortable visiting dimensions that you cited. And somehow I feel like I tripped and fell into this realm this morning.

Voice: Can you accept that you fell and were pushed a bit?

Me: Yes, I just figured that out before you said that. What I am intuiting is that I have an assignment to apprentice to you all and it is connected to the experience of dying?

Voices: Continue.

Me: I agreed to share this information with others in order to bring clarity, compassion and calmness to the dying process.

Voices: You are indeed an accomplished channel. We have chosen well.

Me: (Another long breath) But when I think about the huge sequence of people and events that brought me to this point in time, I am in awe.

Voices: Awe is a good thing. You have been preparing yourself for lifetimes. Do you doubt that you are already ready?

Me: No.

Voices: Know that we will work through you. Trust you will not be overwhelmed. Allow your mind to relax. Continue your prayer practice for it is both an opening and grounding for you. Trust that your human questions will be answered. Return to your writing and feel into the truth of your experience. We will be with you again.

Me: What I know with no clue of how I know it is that Source Code is embedded in our energetic signature, which translates as our frequency. The Source Code remains the same throughout incarnations. Remembering, recovering and returning are our birthright.

Voices: Yes, you are beginning to connect with your mystical nature in a pure and delightful way.

Me: Thank you. I have no need for more words.

August 30th

Today I watched as my light body took over and occluded my physical body. I sat still and attentive, letting go of noting what was happening so I could be more present for the experience. Yet I was attending and remembering without effort and thought "Why not all?" Then I chuckled.

Suddenly, or so it seemed in human time, I was fused with Mary's energy. No longer did I sense my own energy—only Mary's. For an instant I wondered where I had gone. A few times I tried to re-connect with myself mostly to prove to myself that I could. That did not happen.

Mary was all. Mary was Mary. I was Mary. I was experiencing people and the world as Mary, seeing and feeling the pain and suffering and over lighting all of the pain and disease with love, compassion and peace.

What to do with all of this? Why me? Why now? I do acknowledge that I signed up for this adventure, so I will sit with it. When I am doing my strenuous Pilates workout, I reflect about Mary and what it all means and how it is connected to my past life experience. I think there are no simple answers. When I am alone, I breathe into the experience as if re-entering the energy field will bring meaning. So far mystery prevails. I wonder what would happen if I surrender any attachment to making sense of any of this and simply breathed into the unfolding experience. This is a perfect spiritual practice. I will do my best to observe without attachment.

September 2, 2013

This morning before meditation I asked what my Source Code was, not as a signal that I am ready to die, more because I was curious. Even before I had finished framing the question, the answer arrived. So much for cause and effect thinking. I knew on a cellular level, that it was a vortex. Without a second passing, I remembered the first time I saw a vortex. It existed as a freeze frame in my consciousness.

I was about 11 years old and I used to help my grandmother sell penny candy at Mr. Emmons' drug store. On the vortex discovery day, I emptied the sink next to the soda fountain and spotted the downward, rotating spout. I put my finger inside the vortex and felt the swirling movement. I filled the sink several times, released the rubber plug and each time I remember being mesmerized by the shape and the energy of the swirling vortex. I had no name for the phenomena and I could not think of anyone to ask to explain my attraction. Like spider webs, throughout this lifetime I have continued to be fascinated by vortexes.

As I wrote the above paragraph in my journal, without warning, I somersaulted back in time to my friend Darlene's dying time. (I am beginning to appreciate that in quantum time there is no such thing as past, present, and future or even cause and effect.)

I understood now from my expanded perspective that she did not know the way out of her physical body because she did not remember her Source Code. She trusted nothing. Earlier I had channeled the elders of the shamans that she had studied with while in Mexico. I had no clue that "the elders" resided in the Spirit dimension and I expect she did not either. They channeled her auditory Source Code through me and I chanted the ancient code to her. She did not trust them. Although she gave herself permission to navigate going out of her body, with me as guide, she would allow herself to go only so far, get scared and jump back into her body. Memorizing the route without access to her Source Code meant fear overrode intention. When she remembered her Source Code, she was out of here, at last. Just as I wrote the last word, I sensed Darlena around me and heard, "That's right, dear. Thank you, dear friend."

When my friend Richard Harris learned he was dying, he became angry and agitated. He went into resistance, which was a familiar lifetime pattern. When I connected with his guides, they introduced me to his angel. Then I introduced him to his guardian angel and he became less agitated. Looking back, I now believe his angel was his Source Code. His final breath was gentle.

September 6th

I felt as though I was melting like a candle during meditation today. The familiar words that I wrote a year ago on the cover of one of my journals flashed in front of my eyes: Melt me. Mold me. Fill me. Use me. Melting felt distinctly different than blending, merging or fusing. Only my hands felt "whole" and present. The theme of hands continued to intrigue me.

Content to melt, I experienced my light body.

"You were there all the time," I whispered to the air. Then I understood that the "halo" around holy ones was a reflection of their light body and human auras are a combination of human body (thoughts and feelings) and light body.

Then I zoomed into a twenty year old memory of my soul friend Joan Chadbourn's mother, Rose, who refused to die until she had re-built her light body. Since she was not able to speak in the weeks before her death, I interacted with her energetically and relayed messages from her to her family. She became my teacher, as I had never worked with someone who was beyond words. She was very patient and generous with me. She showed me how she withdrew energy from her physical body with her breath and then breathed energy into her light body. I was surprised because I thought our light body was always with us. I had learned that our light body is the realm of conscious co-creation and emergence of planetary healing energies. She was taking no chances. Then she told me she had learned how to revivify her light body long ago when she had enjoyed a lifetime in Egypt. Looking back, I now believe that Rose's Source Code was connected to her light body.

September 11

I had no plan to write the following ideas as I sat down to write in my journal. They spilled out.

Source Code vibrates and pulsates. It is not static. Sometimes one "sees" loved ones on the other side before dying and somehow the re-union sparks a spontaneous memory of their Source Code. Other times remembering Source Code is the green light that alerts "inspirited" loved ones to draw near. In reality all co-exists. It is perception and readiness that determines what is foreground and what is background.

September 15

I understand on an intuitive level that the process of our dying is either a further magnification or merging with our soul story or a grasping to our personal story. It is an epic process—like birth. Some choose to struggle in their personal drama; others choose to merge with their eternal nature. Source Code is an energetic pattern that bridges our consciousness to the next dimension. The light body carries the scintillating energy of our personal Source Code. Source Codes are as unique as soul purpose.

Furthermore, I am learning or re-learning that attaching to human themes of revenge, competition, fear and control can slow down the process of recalling Source Code because the energy field is lowered and the dimming of our light results in scrambledness rather than coherence.

When our ego is in control during dying time, there is fear and holding on to one's personal story. Ego believes that all is lost at death. Therefore ego is unwilling to merge with Source Code.

People familiar with their source Code recognize that dying is a co-creative process

People familiar with their Source Code surrender.

People familiar with their Source Code do not fear dying.

I believe that Steve Jobs was connected to his Source Code and his soul story as he approached death and exclaimed: "Wow! Wow! Wow"!

September 21

During meditation today I gasped when I understood that I had flashed my Source Code prior to being beheaded. I do not have the words to explain how huge a difference this has made to me in terms of integrating and healing the traumatic memories of that lifetime.

Knowing that Mike also, took part in the decision to die while still a teenager puts his life and death in another perspective for me. My sense is that for both of us, it was a soul choice. One of the themes of aligning with soul story is that you become the authority of your inner reality. I have felt a deep peace since putting these pieces together. In a weird way, I can feel both my ego and soul at rest.

I enjoy imagining Source Code as our internal GPS (God Presencing System.) Source Code is not only for your dying time because consciously merging with it while we are alive supports us to fully flourish in our soul story this lifetime.

Since I believe that this information about Source Code is intended for more than me, I intentionally sent out a Thank You to all the other energies that are involved in bringing this information through my consciousness. Then I remember my vow during my vision quest to resume my teaching and to assist others who are ready to dive deep. I am also curious about my three encounters with the mother bear—especially the first time when I convinced myself I might be devoured. Was that event meant as a tipping point for me to re-connect with my Source Code?

I am excited by the far-reaching implications of this information. I, who was sobered by recalling the details of my past lifetime of ecstatic prayer, am now more than captivated by helping people awaken to all they are and that includes their Source Codes. I would stake my life on the validity and reality of this information. My small self recoils. My soul bows.

The few times I have spoken about my exploration about Source Code to friends, I am surprised with their reactions and associations. Here is an example in Georgia Kosciusko's own words,

"In 2011, I was able to visit the site where Archbishop Oscar Romero lived, worked and was assassinated on March 24th, 1980. Three of us from Bangor, Maine went down to accompany peasant refugees who had returned to their communities or needed the presence of "internationals" to have some safety when they gathered.

One of the sisters serving at the hospital described the events of the day he was assassinated, including the fact that Romero would have seen the assassins pull up in front of the doors ready to shoot. He did not stop his sermon until after the bullet took him down.

Georgia spoke in a hushed voice as she continued: "There I was 31 years later after he stood there last feeling a very alive energy envelop my body. It was an experience unlike any other I have had in my life and the power and wisdom of the experience came back to me when Rosie shared her insight about Source Code.

I do not know if the energy I felt in in my body on the grounds of the cancer hospital where Romero worked, lived and died, was tied to Bishop Romero's source code or perhaps a revelation of my own. I do know, however, that I befriend both life and death more fully for myself and others since that experience and I also know in my heart and my body that his spirit lives on not only in the lives of the Salvadorian people, but in the thousands of us who experienced the insight, courage and faith of his people."

I have learned to consult my guides when I wish to have access to a spiritual perspective. I imagine I speed the process up when I send out a Thank You to them even before I am conscious of receiving the information.

> *Voices of Guides: Thank you for catching up! Remembering Source Code is simple. Begin by setting an intention. Then add the energetic feeling of jubilation. Next connect with the hearts and bones of all your ancestors who remembered their unique Source Code upon dying. Prepare to be*

surprised as you discover that your ancestral lineage supports you. It is your intention, your sincerity and your sense of entitlement that determines how easily you remember.

Trying to remember is connected to your ego. Be aware that sometimes your dreams will remind you. Keep a notebook handy to record your dreams because sometime the information will come in layers.

Me: Whew! I have been teaching this retrieval process already.

Voice: Yes, but not with the primary focus of remembering Source Code.

Me: That is true.

Voices: The Source Code retrieval process that we described is both an evolutionary and revolutionary act. Activism has a multitude of forms. You are fast becoming an evolutionary activist.

Me: Cosmic Catalyst is the title I chose for my business card.

Voices: This learning and teaching go way beyond the words on your business card.

Me: I know and just now I wrote "now" instead of know.

Voices: We like "I now."

Me: Whew! This is huge

Voices: Continue to reside in your heart for your heart is vast enough to embrace all that we have spoken and much more.

Me: Yes, thank you, I agree.

> After the channeling, my mind kicked in and gifted me with several practical questions (which I welcomed.)
> What if death is a doorway and the key to open the doorway to your future transformation is your Source Code?
> What if dying could be as simple and natural as breathing?
> What if you consciously remembered how to activate your Source Code when you were ready to die?
> What if you intentionally aligned with your Source Code while living and centered in it when dying?

Since the publication of *Awaken* in 2011, I have done less reading and researching and more experiencing. I am embodying a new way of being in the world—a deeply feminine consciousness combined with a mystical perspective. Direct experience feels like my second heart beat.

I appreciate that I am not the first to write about how we are all awakening to our mystical natures. When I began thinking about this book twenty-two months ago, I did not anticipate ending this book with musing about mysticism. I smile as I acknowledge that God often rests in the surprises. The paradox is that mysticism has been working me since I began journal keeping forty years ago.

Here's how I know:

- I look for unity and recognize intuitively the interconnection of all: people, plants, animals, earth and space.
- I commit to at least one consistent, daily spiritual practice.
- I live in the emerging paradox and participate in the mystery—both the suffering and the joy.
- I appreciate that to be more present in the world means making more room for the world to be present in me.
- I embody an altered appreciation of time and space.
- I embrace simplicity amidst the complexity of daily living.
- I am learning how to embody surrender, non-attachment and compassionate action.
- I am learning about humility and adoration.
- I am learning that goodness is one part of God's heart and one of the secrets of life.
- I envision the future and appreciate the present moment.

Remember that you are the only person who can be a visionary for your own life. I passionately believe that as we give ourselves permission to fully flourish by connecting to our authentic Selves, we recognize that we are not only more than who we ever imagined, but we are even more vast than we are capable of imagining.

Each of us will leave a legacy of love consciousness for future generations. As you claim your entitlement to live even more fully into your emerging soul story, please appreciate that it is your authentic self that empowers and protects you—not the defenses of your ego. As we are touched by the Divine and realize our vast potential, we incorporate the beliefs that have served us in the past.

Evolution erupts and expands when we reach out beyond who we think we are and what we think we are capable of and discover entirely new ways of being, creating and relating. From the sacred space of our soul story, we invite others, dreams, creativity, joy filled service, and God to inform us.

Barbara Marx Hubbard, author of *Emergence,* says it best,

"Conscious Evolution enables us, if we take responsibility for it, to use our creative power to guide our lives and the evolution of the systems and communities in which we live and work. It is a process by which individuals and groups, families, organizations, and societies can envision and create images of what should be and bring those images to life by design."

> Stillness, Compassion and
> Action fuse.
> Leaving an unforgettable after
> taste of eternity.
> Amen

Things To Do

- Recall a moment with God.
- For one week affirm: I am loving awareness. Record your experiences.
- For the next two weeks Promise yourself you will find at least one miracle a day.

Stretching Questions

What is your capacity for being soul centered?
In what ways is your soul purpose connected with love?
What is the biggest risk you have taken in the name of love?
In what ways do you source your Goodness?
What would your life be like if you allowed yourself to love even more outrageously?
What life events have awakened you to your soul story?
What are your spiritual gifts?

♡ Quotations To Take To Heart

"Full faith is grace and it is who you are in essence."
Big Angel

"The true seeker needs to become a pharmacist of bliss.'"
Rumi

"No one was sent into the world without being given the infinite possibilities of the heart." John O' Donahue

"It is our duty to recognize how precious we are and to see all beings as equally precious." Megan Don

"If we want to live from our depths soulfully, then we have to give up all pretenses to innocence." Thomas Moore

Bibliography

Artress, Lauren. Walking A Sacred Path. New York: Riverhead Books, 1995.

Bly, Robert. A Little Book on the Human Shadow. San Francisco: Harper, 1988.

Borysenko, Joan and Dverin, Gordon. Your Soul's Compass. Carlsbad: Hay House, 2007

Bourgeault, Cynthia. Love Is Stronger Than Death. New York: Praxis Publishing, 2007

Braden, Gregg. The Turning Point. California: Hay House, 2014.

Cayce, Edgar. The Psychic Self. Virginia: A.R.E. Press, 2006.

Chopra, Deepak. The Spontaneous Fulfillment of Desire. New York: Harmony Books. 2003.

Daly, Lou Ann. Humans Being. Indiana: Author House, 2009.

Don, Megan. Meditations with Teresa of Avila. California: New World Library, 2005

Dyer, Wayne. Being in Balance. USA: Hay House, 2006.

Gafni, Mark. Your Unique Self. Arizona: Integral Publishers, 2012.

Goddard, Neville, The Neville Reader. California: DeVoss Publications, 1961.

Heart, Deer, Rosalie. Awaken. Indiana: Balboa Press: 2011.

Heart, Deer, Rosalie, Strickland, Alison: Harvesting Your Journals. New Mexico: Heart Link Publications, 1999.

Heart, Deer, Rosalie, Healing Grief. New Mexico: Heart Link Publications, 1996

Hubbard, Marx, Barbara, Emergence: The Shift From Ego to Essence, Virginia: Hampton Roads, 2001.

Kempton, Sally. Awakening Shakti. Colorado: Sounds True, 2013.

McNichols, William, Hart and Starr, Mirabai. Mother of God: Similar to Fire.

New York: Orbis Books, 2010.
McTaggart, Lynne. The Field. Great Britain: HarperColllins. 2001.
Myss, Caroline. Defy Gravity. California: Hay House, 2009.
O'Donahue, John. Beauty. New York: Harper Perennial, 2005.
Palmer, Parker. A Hidden Wholeness: The Journey Toward An Individual Life. Jossey-Bess: USA. 2009.
Plotkin, Bill. Soulcraft. California: New World Library, 2003.
Rilke, Maria Rainer. Letters To A Young Poet. USA: Vintage, 1986.
Rumi, Jel aluddin. The Rumi Collection. USA: Shambhala, 2005.
Spangler, David. The Call. New York: Riverside Books, 1996.
Turrant, John. The Light Inside The Dark. New York: Harper Collins, 1998.
Vaughan, Frances. Awakening Intuition. USA: Anchor Books, 1979.
Whyte. David. What To Remember Upon Waking. USA: Sounds True, 2010.

Book Discussion Guide

Chapter One

Intergenerational family beliefs are powerful determiners of our life—especially those that go unexamined and unchallenged. What are some of your family's life enhancing beliefs and some of your family's life negating beliefs?

Sub-personalities exist in each of us. Rosalie Deer Heart cites examples of clown, victim, rescuer, lover, hero, rock star, and dreamer as examples of sub-personalities. What are your most familiar sub-personalities and what are their gifts to you?

Heart writes that lack of creative expression can lead to depression. Does your experience support or contradict her statement.

Do you agree with the author that how you think about yourself and how you treat others affects your energy field?

Chapter Two

What arises within your consciousness as you consider Buddha's statement, "With our thoughts we create the world."

What roles have shadow wisdom teachers played in your life?

Who, if anyone in your life, might nominate you as a shadow wisdom teacher?

The author introduces the subjects of past lifetimes, karma, and vows as evidence of multi-dimensional consciousness. Do you share her views?

Chapter Three

Do you agree with the author's statement that how you feel about yourself determines what you think is possible?

Carolyn Myss reminds us that learning the power of forgiveness is essential to spiritual growth. What is your most powerful experience with forgiveness?

The author claims that toxic emotions bind us to our personal story. How have toxic emotions played a part in your personal story?

What would you add to the following statement?

Change is the result of consciousness.

Chapter Four

The author writes, "Love is our reason for being and through love every challenge can be transformed into a higher vibration." Do you agree? Why?

How has synchronicity shown up in your life?

Describe a crisis that served as a jumping off place in your life.

Do you believe that quantum thinking, in which all things exist simultaneously, is essential to living into your evolving soul story?

Chapter Five

What are your favorite ways of adding momentum to your intentions?

Do you agree with the author's belief that manifestation is a process of becoming the person whom you can be when the manifestation succeeds?

List a few of your inherited limited beliefs that have compromised your ability to manifest.

What is the most important element of the manifestation process that you plan to remember and implement?

Chapter Six

What is your favorite meditation practice?

When is it the easiest for you to move into the witness state of consciousness?

What causes you to move out of the witness perspective and enter into your personal story?

What benefits have you received from your meditation practice?

Do you agree with the author that meditation is about making connections? Why?

Chapter Seven

In what ways do you experience your intuition?

Do you agree with the author's statement that intuition communicates with us through our imagination? Why?

What was the most recent time that you experienced collaborating with your intuition?

What was your most recent intuitive dream? Did you follow through with action?

Chapter Eight

The author writes that creativity, intuition and healing are interconnected for her. Is that true for you? Explain.

What does your favorite form of creative self-expression ask from you?

What were your family's beliefs about creativity?

Do you agree that solitude is a prerequisite for creativity?

Chapter Nine

Recall some thresholds that you declined to cross. In retrospect are you satisfied that you refused the call?

Has your ego voice ever succeeded in masquerading as your soul voice? What were the consequences?

Do you agree with the author's statement, "Every time I said, "yes" to an aspect of my soul purpose, I merged with an aspect of my future self."

Chapter Ten

Where are you in your journey towards God?

How do you define miracle?

What is an example of a most recent miracle that you have experienced in your life?

Do you agree that faith and miracles are connected? Explain why?

Chapter Eleven

What does the concept of destiny threads mean to you?

Do you believe that destiny threads are part of soul story exclusively or could they also be part of personal story?

In what ways have your soul affiliations supported your growth on your journey?

What are the positive aspects of adopting evolutionary soul buddies? Can you think of possible negative consequences?

Have you identified members of your soul family as a result of reading this chapter? If you have, what is the nature of your agreements?

More Books by Rosalie Deer Heart

Affective Education Guidebook: Activities in the Realm of Feelings with Bob Eberle

Affective Direction: Planning and Feeling for Thinking and Feeling with Bob Eberle

Healing Grief: A Mother's Story

Harvesting Your Journals: Writing Tools to Enhance Your Growth and Creativity with Alison Strickland

Soul Empowerment: A Guidebook For Healing Yourself and Others with Michael Bradford

Celebrating the Soul of CPSI with Dorie Shallcross

Awaken: Awaken Your All Knowing Heart